WEAR
NO
EVIL

HOW TO CHANGE THE WORLD
WITH YOUR WARDROBE

GRETA EAGAN

RUNNING PRESS
PHILADELPHIA · LONDON

Published by Running Press,
A Member of the Perseus Books Group

Books published by Running Press are available at special discounts for bulk purchases in the United States by corporations, institutions, and other organizations. For more information, please contact the Special Markets Department at the Perseus Books Group, 2300 Chestnut Street, Suite 200, Philadelphia, PA 19103, or call (800) 810-4145, ext. 5000, or e-mail special.markets@perseusbooks.com.

ISBN 978-0-7624-5127-2

Library of Congress Control Number: 2014930563

E-book ISBN 978-0-7624-5189-0

9   8   7   6   5   4   3   2   1
Digit on the right indicates the number of this printing

Designed by Joshua McDonnell
Edited by Cindy De La Hoz
Typography: Avenir, Bembo, and Lato
Illustrator: Natasha Landenberger

Running Press Book Publishers
2300 Chestnut Street
Philadelphia, PA 19103-4371

Visit us on the web!
www.runningpress.com

To my dearest family and friends,

who asked me about my dreams and

supported me in fulfilling them.

CONTENTS

INTRODUCTION

See no evil. Hear no evil. Speak no evil. *Wear* no evil. From tragic textile-related head-lines to icy editors, it is easy to group all of fashion into the evil column. Yet with its wide reach and influence, fashion has a rightful place in our evolution as global citizens and as ambassadors to a sustainable and just future for generations to come. Odds are that if you picked up this book, you too are wondering where doing good and looking good come together. My hope is that this book will guide your awareness and your actions, because small steps add up to big shifts.

Paraphrasing a speech by President Barack Obama, in which he said something that resonated deeply within me: our actions today impact the world of tomorrow. In other words, we have a choice to play an active role in the world we create and leave behind for our children. That is why I wrote this book, and that is why you are reading it.

Of course, I didn't always share that belief. I made my way through life blind to the impact of my purchases for my first twenty years of life. But let's start from the begin-ning. My journey into the world of fashion and style started as early as I can remember. My great-grandmother, Grammy Bea (short for Beatrice, the name I always wanted des-perately to inherit), was a model and married a prominent banker in San Francisco. I remember visiting them as a child in what we called the "Golden Apartment," where I wasn't allowed to touch anything. Everything had a perfected placement and gilded pres-ence. At her husband's request she would host important businessmen for cocktails and dinner, and inevitably she developed a classic 1960s style. Her sheath dresses, oversized jewelry, and coral lipstick made a lasting impression. Next, my Auntie Holly followed in Bea's footsteps and also became a model. She learned the tricks of the trade and devel-oped her own personal style. A few years after graduating high school she opened a cos-metics boutique in the Bay Area, where she assisted women in selecting their ideal colors and helped them discover how to highlight their best features.

As for my mother (Holly's kid sister), she grew up during the hippie age and believed only in peace, love, and macramé. She married my father at a young age, and they spent their honeymoon in the infamous dude ranch town of Jackson Hole, Wyoming. Many years later we children were raised there, competing in barrel racing, ice skating, and Nordic skiing. It was a wonderful athletic playground, but not so big in the way of fashion. Yet a sartorialist cannot be stopped, no matter how po-dunk and rural their surroundings! So I would casually add an *Allure* magazine or *Teen Vogue* to the checkout line when my mom took me grocery shopping. Every birthday someone would tap into my thirst for beauty and fashion how-to books, and I would devour them within the day of receiving them. And then there was Auntie Holly. Unfortunately Grammy Bea didn't live long enough to see me develop into a young woman or even a teenager. But Auntie Holly was there to pass the torch.

She would send boxes of product samples. I had a cornucopia of colors to choose from for lips, eyes, cheeks, and nails. I experimented with everything and diligently followed my various beauty books' advice on how to apply certain colors for specific skin, hair, and eye color combos. I'd host sleepovers at which my friends would line up to have me pluck their eyebrows. And so it went all four years of my high school career.

I became the girl who anyone within my circle consulted for a new haircut or color, their prom dress, what to wear to their sister's wedding, and how to create a plentiful and functioning wardrobe. I think my crowning glory was my junior year, when I wore a silver brocade pant set (a strapless top with streamlined cigarette trousers) to our winter formal and was named WinterBall Queen. I was stunned. I knew my place as a style adviser to my friends and family, but I had no idea the rest of the school considered me an arbiter of style.

As you can tell by now, the fashion lover's blood has been flowing through me for quite some time. And even though I fought it (I studied sports pre-med for undergrad before switching to fashion for graduate school), I never could keep those tips and tricks I picked up along the way from echoing in the back of my mind before lending my advice on a friend's style conundrum.

And as I entered into the fashion world full time, a funny thing happened: my conscience got checked—hard. I would make small, conscious decisions about the food I put into my body but not the creams I put on my body or the clothes I wore next to my body. My conscience check was much less about the ceaseless desire for wanting material things and more to do with what I was supporting by being both a consumer and proprietor of fashion.

During my studies at the London College of Fashion I was required to do a work placement. My first work placement lasted six months and was with a talented and independent Central Saint Martins graduate designer named Jane Carr. Her work ethic, ingenuity, and sheer dedication were a priceless influence on my life. Yet I longed to see what it was like with the big brands. And so I took another work placement the following year at a major internationally recognized label. (I won't disclose this brand's name because it could have been any major brand—many of them operate the same way.) This turned out not to be as rosy as I had envisioned, and I grudgingly made it through my four-month agreement. Although it was one of the toughest times in my life, I am forever grateful for that difficult experience because it opened my eyes and taught me what I *didn't* want.

It was at this fashion house that I learned the dirty secrets behind luxury's deceptive luster. Samples for the upcoming collections would be shipped in from China and sectioned off into mounting piles of "potential" products. They reeked of toxic dyes and glues, and more often than not they would fall apart before the week's end as they were tried on for fit and aesthetic. I remember feeling disturbed somewhere deep down inside when we would sit through meetings and select pieces from the piles to present as a potential item that would go into production. There was so much. And so much waste. And while the other interns gushed and excitedly interjected their opinions, I sunk into a lonely place where my conscience sat patiently waiting for me. That was a dark time for me. I was confronted on one hand with my personal values and ideals for the world I wanted to be an active citizen of and, on the other, what felt like the only reality for having a career in fashion—a shallow and recklessly wasteful existence.

I began to wonder: Could there be a real movement toward fashion with ethics? Fashion and style without the evil that drives corporate culture and destroys our planet? Could we look as good but hurt the world less?

You see, this book isn't about giving up style to live a greener life. Who wants that?

I was a fashion lover long before I became an environmentalist (even though deep down I always cared). The truth is that I care about how I look and feel, and I know you do too. I don't discount the importance of the confidence that looking good or doing good brings; I just don't think that style and sustainability are mutually exclusive. They sit at equal weight, and by reading this book you'll learn they can live in harmony. What is really necessary is a reboot. We need to restart the conversation around fashion—how it is produced, consumed, and discarded—to fit with the world we live in today. Pretty simple, right? It will be, once you've read this book.

This book is about navigating the new frontier of responsible fashion in a way that lets your sartorial heart sing with a clear and uplifted conscience, as you re-enter the world knowing how to *wear* no evil. Are you ready to become an ambassador to style with substance? I know you are. Let's get started!

HOW TO USE THIS BOOK

My hope is that you will use this book as your *wear no evil* handbook. I find that a lot of people have the best intentions when it comes to aligning their wardrobe with their values, but without a road map, they give up and buy what is easy (and not ethical) or they opt out and don't purchase the items they truly need for fear of supporting production methods they don't believe in. I have watched too many people around me sacrifice, either on the style or ethics front, and they needn't! There are so many options and so many flexible ways to navigate this new frontier of fashion, where style and sustainability coincide.

So let's get down to it! This book is divided into three parts. The first section provides a little insight into why we should care about where our clothes come from and the impact the fashion industry is having on the world. Then we go straight to the toolbox, where I break down all of the ways a piece of fashion can be considered eco with my exclusive Integrity Index. Next you'll learn how to incorporate those integrity ratings into the Diamond Diagram for a go-anywhere guide to fashion with ethics.

The second part is all about building your fashion foundation. I'll cover color ways and body type, then move into a closet-cleansing exercise, and give you tons of tips on how to discard your giveaway pile properly and to organize your closet. Next you'll read through style suggestions for every area of your collective wardrobe. In each category you'll find style advice, a green guide to shopping for these key items, and a list of suggested brands to purchase, ranked by integrity rating, diamond level, and price.

The last part rounds out your wear-no-evil makeover with example outfits on what to wear to various occasions (which include the same integrity and diamond ratings established in Part One). Lastly, get ready to groom with nontoxic beauty suggestions and guidance to complete your transformation into a consciously cool consumer.

The beauty of this book is that you can take as much or as little as you need from it to make it work in your life with your personal style. Once you have a solid grasp on the Integrity Index and Diamond Diagram, the sky is the limit as to where you can shop. The style suggestions I make are just that—suggestions. They are style staples I've found to work well in my life and have also been recommended by various stylists, editors, and style icons. The best part about fashion is that it is individual. How you dress communicates who you are—both on the style and ethics front—and is completely unique to you. This book will make the delivery of that message that much easier.

With that said, turn the page, and welcome to the future of fashion!

xx,

Greta

P.S. You can check out LiveNoEvil.com for the most up-to-date Wear No Evil inspiration and resources.

PART
1

CHAPTER 1

TO WEAR OR NOT TO WEAR?

"Clothes make the man. Naked people have little or no influence on society."

—MARK TWAIN

Every day we make two decisions that have an enormous impact on the world around us: what to eat and what to wear. With help from successful books like *The Omnivore's Dilemma* and the popularity of Whole Foods and the Slow Food Movement, we've begun to overcome the first challenge. USDA-approved organic, Fair Trade, non-GMO, and local have all become common qualifiers for our grocery shopping habits. When it comes to food, we can confidently shop, knowing that the items we purchase fall in line with who we are—you are what you eat—and what we support.

But what about the second challenge? Maybe you hadn't yet realized that the simple question—to wear or not to wear?—truly is a multifaceted dilemma. Obviously, the first part of that tricky question is to decide whether what you've selected to wear accurately represents your style. The importance of style is not to be underrated, because whether you admit it or not, it plays a role in your everyday life and tells the world what you think of yourself and what others should think of you. I love what Miuccia Prada said about style: "What you wear is how you present yourself to the world, especially today, when human contacts are so quick. Fashion is instant language."[1]

Yet there is another side to consider when getting dressed. Does this outfit reflect my values and who I am as well as my personal style? And there's the rub! Until recently not many of us ever considered the second side of that daily question: What *should* I wear today?

When I moved out of my small hometown in Wyoming to the fabulously fashion-forward city of London, my sole focus was to find pieces to build my wardrobe. I was on the hunt for clothing that suited my lifestyle and embodied my developing identity as a career woman in fashion. I was completely clueless about checking where the pieces were made, what the materials were made of, and whether I thought the price could possibly reflect a fair wage for production. And although ethics were on my radar in other realms—like food, transport, energy and water conservation, and recycling—it simply never occurred to me that those same ethics could and *should* extend to include my wardrobe. Well, we all know that they eventually did, and I've shared that turning point with you already. And very gradually I've watched as those around me and in the news, magazine features, on red carpets, and runways have all begun to express a desire to merge ethics with style too.

A lot of that stirred motivation is a reflection of the terrible consequences from fashion that are more and more visible and apparent. Today, you can't watch the news without seeing stories about the sweatshops in Southeast Asia, tragic fires or structural collapses in unsafe clothing factories, or deadly dyes and unregulated pollution silently seeping their ways across India and China. Not to mention the lost jobs that have been outsourced to poverty-stricken children halfway across the globe.

How did we get here?

Of course, fashion didn't start this way. Clothing came from a place of necessity, even in our classic closet staples: Blue jeans were produced to give mining workers in California a sturdy and durable pair of pants to work in. The flapper dresses of the 1920s gave women more flexibility in their movements and comfort. The trench coat gave British soldiers in the trenches during World War II a functional jacket that could hold grenades on their belt and protect them from the elements.

The great leaders of fashion—Coco Chanel, Christian Dior, Louis Vuitton, the Hermes family—built the foundation for modern-day fashion by exploring form and function while upholding quality and craft. They produced wares for the wealthy, famous, and royal. To own and wear fashionable pieces was a social-class signifier that only the economically elite could afford. Before the 1900s most people had a handful of garments in their closets that were constantly being repaired and passed down. Even in the twenties the average middle-class American woman had nine outfits (total, each year) that she would lovingly care for and wear week after week.[2]

It wasn't until the 1950s and 1960s that income and advertising took off, changing the fashion industry forever. After World War II, men and women were actively in the workplace, earning dual incomes for a single-family household. Still concerned with social status and clothing as an indicator, men and women alike "traded up" by purchasing discounted quality-made and designer-label clothing in bargain basements. According to Elizabeth Cline, author of *Overdressed: The Shockingly High Cost of Cheap Fashion,* the 1960s was when clothing turned away from necessity and the idea of "keeping up with the latest fashions" came into play. Big-brand department stores popped up around the United States, and Sears notoriously sent out its catalog to the picket-fenced homes of America.

In the late sixties and early seventies, counterculture abolished any outer display of wealth, and conspicuous consumption faded into the background. It wasn't until around the 1980s, when working women with disposable income came into vogue, that the opulent show of luxury reemerged. Greater mobility along the socioeconomic ladder opened the marketplace to a greater audience who could participate in luxury at various levels. This proved a pointed shift for the luxury fashion sector, soon to be followed by mainstream mass-market retailers.

Corporate tycoons gobbled up the luxury fashion houses that had been established and run by the founding families, turning them into dominating international brands listed on the world's stock exchanges.[3] They sold a capitalist agenda disguised as "the democratization" of fashion, which would make luxury accessible to all. Even if they believed their own hype, the very ethos of artisan-crafted clothing and accessories, which warrant a luxury price tag, often went out the window when luxury companies went public.

"Going public does force you to change the way you do business. It forces you to be aware of how you are spending and where it's going, to make some short-term decisions because that's what shareholders respond to," stated Tom Ford (formerly a lead designer at Gucci) in an interview with Dana Thomas for her book *Deluxe: How Luxury Lost Its Luster.* Translation: luxury brands cut corners. They outsourced production, used cheaper materials, and employed rock-bottom manufacturing to turn the biggest profit. Coach was one of the first brands to take its production out of the local New York garment district and use Chinese factories and labor to produce their goods. Their successful experience with production in the Far East prompted a colossal migration of other US- and European-based luxury brands.

Meanwhile, during the 1990s and early 2000s, mass fashion retailers like Spain's Zara and Sweden's H&M were developing the business model of fast fashion. They pioneered a corporate retail model that boasted fast-paced consumption in response to constantly changing styles. By keeping their production nearby their design offices and markets, they were able to capitalize on quick turnaround and had the ability to make last-minute changes. Yet in order to pull it off, they rely on volume and push production and consumption to unsustainable scales. Zara reportedly produces 1 million garments a day![4] Their "cheap and cheerful" prices for trendy clothes prompted an entirely new category of clothing: disposable fashion. Fashion-obsessed men and women would purchase fast fashion on a weekly, if not daily, basis to update their wardrobes and ensure they weren't caught wearing the same thing twice.

By 2011 the average American was purchasing sixty-eight new wardrobe items a year—double what we had been purchasing in 1991.[5] Who has the closet space for that much clothing? None of us do, and so Americans throw out an average of sixty-eight pounds of clothing each year, which amounts to 13.1 million tons of textile waste that goes to US landfills each and every year.[6] The craziest part is that 95 percent of that waste is, in fact, recyclable.[7] We are literally throwing away valuable resources while simultaneously existing in a world where we have limited resources. It doesn't add up.

BRACE FOR IMPACT

I hate to say it, but the environmental and inhumane impact of such irresponsible production and consumption is as bad as you think it is. Brace yourself. This is the part where I give you some tough facts to convince your ego to start listening to your conscience and supply you with heavy-hitting material to back your position when speaking to those around you about your hip transition to being a conscious consumer.

According to the World Wildlife Fund's 2012 Living Planet Report, 40 percent of the world's population live in river basin areas that experience droughts and severe water scarcity at least one month per year. That may have something to do with the fact that the average T-shirt takes seven hundred gallons of water to produce. For just one shirt! Magnify that water use for a single item across the global textile industry, and it is easy (yet still alarming) to see that the textile industry uses 100 million gallons of water annually.[8]

In 2012 Global Trends 2030 reported that annual global water requirements will hit 6,900 billion cubic meters by 2030, which is 40 percent above current sustainable water supply levels. It is essentially like buying on credit. We're living a lifestyle we can't actually afford, and so we just "put it on our tab" and think that we will deal with it later, but we are talking about water here, people—a necessity for life! The next time you buy a pair of jeans, it might be worth a second thought as to whether you would actually prefer the drinking water it took to make them—about eighteen hundred gallons per pair.[9] Sounds scary when put into that context, but 2030 is not that far away.

Water use by the fashion industry is as intensive as it is dirty. Chemical solvents and toxic dyes are readily used in heaping amounts and spewed into natural waterways without properly being treated. By now, most of us have heard of the Greenpeace Detox Campaign (launched in April 2012). Greenpeace purchased clothing from twenty major fashion brands and then ran tests to determine their toxicity levels. According to their findings, "All of the samples were tested for the concentration of NPEs (nonylphenol ethoxylates). Once released to the environment, NPEs degrade to nonylphenol, which is known to be toxic primarily due to being a hormone disruptor—persistent and bioaccumulative (known to accumulate in living organisms). Garments that were dyed were tested for the presence of carcinogenic amines that are released from certain azo dyes used to dye fabric. The thirty-one garments bearing a plastisol print were also tested for phthalate esters (commonly referred to as phthalates)."[10]

Of the 141 articles of clothing purchased for this study, 89 were found to contain NPEs. Phthalates were detected in all 31 samples with plastisol-printed fabric. Two of the samples made by manufacturers for Zara tested positive for the presence of azo dyes, which release cancer-causing amines.[11]

Okay, let's pull all of this heavy-hitting information together. Major fashion brands, whose clothing winds up all over the world, are using manufacturers in areas where the use of NPEs are not illegal (second- and third-world countries) and where toxic dyes are still blindly permitted. Essentially, even environmentally aware and educated countries that have governmental policies in place to protect the people and the planet are subjected to toxic chemicals that have been shown to cause cancer and disrupt normal hormone activity (causing feminization and other hormonal irregularities) because of retail import practices.

That means that you can buy a cute and cheap top from one of your favorite fashion brands and not only will you be wearing those chemicals close to your skin, but when you wash them, they are released into our home water systems. I'm not one for naming and shaming, but thank goodness Greenpeace is and decided to bring this all to the forefront with their Zero Hazardous Waste campaign. Luckily, the fashion brands they called out, and others that weren't included but self-volunteered, took the pledge for zero hazardous waste by 2020.

Unfortunately, focusing on chemicals solely in our waterways would be too limited a scope for the damage the textile industry does. Land use and the cultivation of crops as fibers have an important place in textile production. Cotton, also known as white gold, has long been both a celebrated and vilified crop. Not only is cotton one of the thirstiest crops, conventional cotton is also pesticide laden. Approximately $2 billion worth of chemicals are sprayed on cotton crops worldwide every year, half of which are designated toxic by the World Health Organization.[12]

Farmers' exposure to herbicides, fertilizers, pesticides, and growth regulators have caused occupational illnesses and pesticide poisonings that amount to 3 million cases per year, resulting in twenty thousand poisoning deaths.[13] Not only do the workers and farmers directly exposed to these chemicals suffer, but the land also accumulates these toxins like compound interest in a bank account. The result is soil toxicity, which makes growing crops harder and releases chemical run-off into our waterways. In addition, the textile industry affects the quality of soil, as farmers try to keep up with demand and plant the same crop season after season, depleting biodiversity and natural crop rotation integral to soil health.

Land use, in general, is a rather contentious topic and one that held center stage at the World Economic Forum (WEF) in January 2012. In their industry agenda WEF reported that "Unless the present link between growth and consumption of scarce resources is severed, our resource base, governance, and policy structures are unlikely to sustain the standard of living societies have grown accustomed to and aspire to."[14] In other words, we are at a critical tipping point at which world leaders are no longer concerned about securing basic necessities (like food and water) to those in developing countries, but for the world at large. Forests are cleared to create crop fields, not for food. Countries that were once agriculturally independent have shifted to produce textile crops or raise livestock, and they now import food. This uncalculated misuse of natural resources and land is multifaceted.

Animal rights activists argue that if all the land used for livestock was instead used to grow grains and vegetables, we could feed the world three times over. And that doesn't even touch the humanity side of things. PETA (People for the Ethical Treatment of Animals) openly displays the underbelly of the clothing industry and its unethical use of animals. Every year millions of animals are mistreated and killed—all in the name of fashion.[15] The leather industry alone is responsible for slaughtering over a billion animals a year.[16] On PETA's website they state that "Many of these animals suffer all the horrors of factory farming—including extreme crowding and confinement, deprivation, and unanesthetized castration, branding, tail-docking, and *dehorning*—as well as cruel treatment during transport and slaughter." And the negative effects don't stop there.

The tanning of leather takes its toll on our environment too. Most US leather producers and those around the world use a chrome-tanning technique that outputs chromium as a byproduct into our waterways and soil. The Environmental Protection Agency (EPA) considers chromium-containing waste hazardous.[17] The Center for Disease Control (CDC) found, for example, that leukemia cases were five times higher than the national average in residents near a tannery in Kentucky.[18]

Raising livestock is also energy and resource intensive. Overstocking of animals is common and leads to soil deterioration and eventual desertification of the land previously used. Over the last 250 years, manure and its associated methane gas from cattle, sheep, and other animals raised for their fur and meat has greatly contributed to an increase in greenhouse gasses and global warming.[19] It turns out that passing gas is more serious than just a smelly situation. And the stench doesn't stop there. Our carbon emissions are drastically connected to global warming and the environmental changes we are beginning to understand and experience.

CarbonTrust.com issued an annual report on the international carbon flows of clothing, which stated that "The global production of clothing results in around 330MtCO$_2$ being produced annually, which is about 1.2 percent of global human CO$_2$ production emissions. In-use emissions from clothing, principally arising from washing and drying, but also including ironing and dry-cleaning, cause a further ~530MtCO$_2$ to be emitted, equivalent to around 2 percent of global emissions."[20] If we put that into context (and add the other CO$_2$ sectors that make up the total CO$_2$ emissions of the fashion industry), the apparel and textile industry comes in second on a scale of highest CO$_2$ emissions, with 2.1 million tons produced annually, just behind the petroleum industry.

If you've ever been to China, you've had a firsthand experience with the pollution that makes almost every day foggy and overcast. Perched atop a mountain crest on a hike just outside of central Hong Kong in 2013, I looked down at the tightly packed city and had a sense of vertigo from the pollution distortion. And, of course, the mere mention of China brings us to yet another issue within the fashion industry—the fair and ethical treatment of people.

Under the leadership of Deng Xiaopeng in 1978, China named four "special export zones" and then seized the opportunity to create a source of GDP through the use of its plentiful land and workers by setting up factories. In doing so China thus redrew the global manufacturing map.[21] Hundreds of thousands of rural citizens moved into factory cities in hopes of finding a job where they could work with their head down for a couple of years, save money, and return home with finances to invest in themselves and their children's education. They didn't question the safety of their workplaces (or, rather, lack thereof) and welcomed the long hours and option to add overtime to their paychecks.

Today most of the factory workers are women, aged sixteen to twenty-five. There are dorms set up on the factory grounds that they share ten to twelve per room with same-sex bathrooms that are typically avoided because of the stench.[22] They work long hours in assembly-line production, collapsing with fatigue at the end of their sometimes eighteen-hour days. The government doesn't strictly enforce limited work hours or safety regulations because economic growth is the country's top priority, even at the cost of its people's health and well-being. Each year over 200 million Chinese workers across 16 million companies are subjected to dangerous working conditions. In 2005 China recorded 665,043 cases of occupational illness (usually a lung disease that takes its hold over time and is known as a silent killer).[23]

The workers are rarely warned of the dangers associated with the factory work they've agreed to do nor are they equipped with proper safety gear or instructions. Instead of installing ventilation systems to help disperse toxic fumes and dust particles, the factories often seal in their hazardous pollutants by keeping the doors and windows shut tight to the outside world to stay beneath the radar of pollution regulators.

Of course, there are factory audits in which health inspectors and company representatives (from Walmart and the like) make their rounds. The Chinese are prepared. They have what are deemed "demonstration factories" that meet the government and employing retailer's health and safety requirements. At these "five-star factories," the factory managers confidently tour officials, who then return their reports with satisfactory seals of approval. Yet for every five-star demonstration factory there are any number of shadow factories located a few miles away doing the real work under an unregulated veil necessary to produce goods at the price points Western retailers have come to expect and demand.

In 2007 production costs for luxury items made in China were 30 to 40 percent less than those made in Italy.[24] The profit savings is a combination of cheaper materials and cheaper labor. According to the Bureau of Statistics in 2011, the average Chinese worker made one-tenth the wage of their standard American counterpart ($1.36 per hour to our $23.32 hourly rate). Consequently, 2.8 million US jobs have been replaced with Chinese labor despite the higher skill and productivity levels of US employees.[25]

The race to the zero (or the cheapest production costs) doesn't end in China. The pressure to uphold environmental standards for production and increase wages while decreasing working hours in China has shifted fashion production to other, even cheaper countries like India, Vietnam, and Myanmar. Today Bangladesh employs 3.5 million people in the garment and textile sector, accounting for 79 percent of its total exports.[26] Unfortunately, working conditions in India aren't any better than those in China. In 2013 a tragic fire at the Walmart-linked Tazreen Fashion factory in Dhaka claimed 117 lives and injured another 200 because of an unsafe environment without proper evacuation exits and routines. Sadly, that served as a precursor to the even more devastating Tazreen factory collapse that claimed over a thousand lives. Additionally, India's use of underage workers has earned it a shameful title as the capital of child labor. Lucy Siegle reports in her book *To Die For: Is Fashion Wearing Out the World?* that children as young as five years old are adept with a needle, and their small hands are often responsible for the intricate beadwork found on cheap fashion tops.

Stories about child labor, unethical treatment of people and animals, and the blatant disregard for limited resources coupled with the abuse of our environment could and have filled many books. And although I have given you some fodder for your ethical arguments (both intrinsic and external), this book is not another one of those journalistic books that peels back the glamorous veil of fashion to reveal its unkept underbelly. If you crave more stats and stories, I absolutely encourage you to check out the sources I have cited in this section. You will learn more than you thought possible about the way the fashion industry works and the real costs of "affordable" goods.

This book, however, is a call to action that comes after the awakening. If you are reading this, it is reasonable to assume that you care about the earth we call home and the living beings upon it. You are likely already educated to a degree that has influence over the products you choose to buy and use, and you are operating on a "green" level in other areas of your life (e.g., transportation, energy conservation, etc.). Yet you picked up this book because you recognize that there is a disconnect between your values (and how you spend your money to support certain brands and organizations) and the very clothes you wear to help communicate who you are.

It would be easy to blame our current state of irresponsible fashion production on the brands, manufacturers, and retailers, but it would not be entirely fair. The fact of the matter is that we are in this together. As consumers, we vote with our dollars and tell the brands what we want and at what price we are willing to pay for it. This is both a dangerous (as we've found out) and simultaneously empowering position. When we decide what our limits, boundaries, and ideals are and then collectively communicate them through our purchasing habits, we impart change. And with that action we begin to realize the words of Ghandi: "Be the change you want to see in the world."

The truth is that fashion needs a reboot. For an industry that is obsessed with what's new, it is a little ironic that its actual mode of production, use, and waste management is seriously outdated. As so many other industries are finding greater efficiencies in closed-loop cycles, renewable resources and energy, recycling, and technology, fashion, for the most part, has stayed stagnant. Why? Probably because they figure if it isn't broken, don't fix it. But I guess they didn't get the memo: it is broken—severely. Luckily, that little sticky note of change is being passed around, and its influence is spreading.

Around the world and across all industries—food, automobiles, construction, beauty, and so forth—we are beginning to recognize that a more deliberate, intelligent, and responsible approach is necessary. Fashion is the last frontier.

You can only turn a blind eye for so long while your conscience gently pulls at you, and then you cross over into a space where you know too much and are too good of a person (thank heavens!) to just let it slide. Hi, and welcome to the future of fashion. Don't be dismayed. It is getting easier all the time to satisfy your sartorial self as well as your conscience. In fact, one day—perhaps not too far off—we won't need to classify this kind of fashion as eco or sustainable because everything will just be ethically sourced and sustainably produced in fashion. But until that day comes, this book will guide you through a transition that is seamless and unmistakably stylish.

ECO-FASHION: AWAKENING THE CONSCIOUS CONSUMER

There is no denying that we are in the throes of "The Green Movement." Green energy, green buildings, green (electric or hybrid) cars, green cleaning products—you get the picture. And, you guessed it, there is most certainly a thing called green fashion. But this is where it gets a little confusing, because green fashion also flies under the alias of eco-fashion, sustainable fashion, ethical fashion, slow fashion, responsible fashion, style with substance . . . and there are more hip and chic titles propagated by word-smithing journalists every day. Let me simplify it for you. They all mean the same thing. For the most part these varying terms are more reflective of where they are used: In the United States we like to call it green or eco-fashion, most of Europe is hooked on the term slow fashion, and in the UK they are particularly keen on addressing it as ethical fashion. No matter where in the world you reside, the underlying essence is that the fashion you are speaking of is considered. Okay, now I am throwing yet another word at you, but the word "considered" makes the most sense to me.

In interviews I am often asked how I define eco-fashion. I think it was an Earth Day interview I did for the *Net-a-Porter* online magazine when I finally hit upon a concise and accurate way of describing it. Eco-fashion is considered fashion. The production, materials, people, and planet are all considered as well as the generations to come. I'll break that simple statement down into greater detail when we look at the Integrity Index (Chapter 2), but for now we can think of it as the catchy first line on a résumé of an applicant whom we are just getting to know.

And where did this worldly applicant come from, you may ask? Well, if we get-holier-than-thou about it, eco-fashion has been here since the beginning. And even though it feels snobby to say such a thing, that is the truth. The way clothing production started was very sustainable. It started at the hands of skilled men and women who devoted their lives to their craft—reusing materials, patching pieces, dyeing with natural pigments they found in the fruit, vegetation, and soil around them, and carefully tailoring the fit and passing items down. But I don't want to spend the entire book bringing us up to present day, so let's jump forward and pick up the storyline when modern-day eco-fashion, as a term and category, came onto the fashion world's radar.

MODERN "ECO" FASHION TIMELINE

1970s

Eco-fashion first appears as part of the modern environmental movement. It is associated with the hippie culture's emphasis on self-sufficiency, chemical-free dyes, and natural textiles.[27] Eco-fashion generally consists of secondhand clothing and handcrafted designs.[28]

1974: The British charity Oxfam begins selling handicrafts sourced directly from small producers abroad and launches a recycling center for clothing donations.[29]

1979: Traidcraft is established, seeking to end poverty through trade.[30]

1980s

1980: PETA is founded, leading antifur and antileather campaigns in the United States.[31]

1983: Katharine Hamnett launches the world's first slogan T-shirts—reinforcing the connection between clothing choices and sociopolitical messages.[32]

1988: Martin Margiela launches the first collection featuring repurposed materials and soon spearheads the deconstructivist movement for his use of recycled materials.[33]

1990s

Eco-fashion as a term is out there and being used primarily by environmentalists who are creating clothing that is eco-friendly. They sought to produce clothing without the use of pesticides, instead using natural dyes and with simplicity in mind. Unfortunately, this is where and when eco-fashion got a bad rap. For the most part eco-fashion was being "designed" and produced by environmentalists who didn't have any training in or perhaps even an eye for—sorry to be harsh, but someone had to say it—design. So we wound up with a lot of frumpy, earth-toned, shapeless T-shirts and "yoga" pants. Even Calvin Klein got in on the first eco-fashion wave, but the supply chains for organic cotton were weak, so he didn't have many options, and inevitably the clothing came out looking dull and like loungewear basics for a beach holiday.

March 1990: For the first time, *Vogue* addresses eco-fashion in the article "Natural Selection."[34]

June 1990: Members of the Fashion Group, including Katharine Hamnett, discuss the impact of fashion production with the United Nations.[35]

1994: Esprit launches a range of ecological clothing focusing on sustainable materials and ethical production.[36]

1995: Giorgio Armani introduces hemp textiles into his Emporio Armani collection.[37]

late 1990s: Various reports expose sweatshop labor in fashion supply chains, spurring consumer pressure on fashion brands and retailers to implement factory compliance and monitoring programs.[38]

1998: The Ethical Trading Initiative is established to improve labor practices of global supply chains.[39]

2000–2009

Eco-fashion is on the rise. The industry is finally starting to outgrow its stigma as the sole producers of ill-fitting, beige, hemp T-shirts. Conferences around the globe, in Germany, France, Spain, the UK, Australia, Sweden, and the United States are popping up to discuss this thing called eco-fashion and showcase its designers. Esthetica, founded in 2006 by the British Fashion Council, becomes a staple at London Fashion Week, where designers grab media attention and move eco-fashion into the limelight.

2000: *No Logo* by Naomi Klein is published, drawing further media and consumer attention to the realities of international corporate business practices in the fashion industry. Consumer demand for corporate social responsibility related to sustainability and ethical trading grows.[40]

2001: Stella McCartney launches her brand, using only animal-friendly materials.[41]

2002: Trash Couture, based out of Denmark, is established, using recycled couture fabrics and vintage lace.[42]

2004: Gucci volunteers for supply-chain assessment in demonstration of corporate social responsibility.[43]

2004: The first Ethical Fashion Show is held in Paris, showcasing sustainable artisanal design.[44]

2004: The first Fairtrade minimum prices for cotton are issued by Fairtrade International.[45]

March 2005: U2's Bono and his wife, Ali Hewson, create the socially linked fashion brand Edun, and it is featured in *Vogue*.[46]

2005: Linda Loudermilk launches her luxury sustainable fashion label and trademarks the term eco-luxury.[47]

2006: The British Fashion Council launches Estethica at London Fashion Week.[48]

April 2007: Anya Hindmarch's "I'm Not a Plastic Bag" shopping totes sell out within an hour in London.[49]

October 2007: Portland Fashion Week premiers the first all-green fashion week in the world.[50]

November 2007: Rogan Gregory (also a cofounder of the brand Edun) is awarded the prestigious CFDA/*Vogue* Fashion Fund Award.[51]

January 2008: Earth Pledge and Barney's New York present FutureFashion, a runway show featuring sustainable designs from leading names such as Versace, Calvin Klein, and Yves Saint Laurent.

2009: Livia Firth (Collin Firth's wife) spearheads the Green Carpet Challenge, bringing A-list celebrities and brands together to celebrate sustainability and style at some of the most prestigious red-carpet awards ceremonies.

June 2009: This month's *Vogue* is themed around eco-fashion.[52]

October 2009: *Women's Wear Daily* reports that consumers are "ready to go eco."[53]

2010–2011

Mainstream is paying attention, and fashion authorities such a *Marie Claire* and *Elle* magazines are openly discussing the ideas behind eco-fashion as well as the brands committed to it. Big brands are jumping on the green bandwagon and producing eco-friendly lines. H&M announces its Conscious Collection, made of recycled and organic materials. Top Shop sets out its ReClaim to Wear line, which is made from upcycled fabric. Levi's releases its Water<Less jeans, which use 96 percent less water. Eco-fashion- and eco-beauty-specific magazines come into publication, including *Recognise*, *Sublime*, and *Ethical Consumer* in the UK and *CocoEco* in the United States.

February 2010: New York Fashion Week initiates a carbon-neutral policy.[54]

September 2010: London Fashion Week stages its first official sustainable fashion show.[55]

March 2011: *Vogue* and Christie's collaborate with Runway to Green to host an eco-fashion show and live auction.[56]

July 2011: Eco-fashion brand Suno is named CFDA/*Vogue* Fashion Fund finalist.[57]

2012+

Public interest and awareness is growing, and brands are taking note. Greenpeace issues a report that declares Zara the top producer of toxic clothing. Zara, Mango, Levi's, and others vow to clean up their clothing and hit zero hazardous waste by 2020. Walmart announces it will supply one hundred thousand jobs to US veterans and invest $1 billion in US-made goods over the next three years. Natalia Allan, a Parsons graduate, helps pioneer the new frontier in fashion with a 3-D clothing printer and literally "prints" clothes with a zero waste process. Textile recycling gains momentum, as those in the industry recognize the billion-dollar savings in closed-loop cycles. H&M launches the iCollect program, where the public is invited to drop off bags of discarded clothing (inclusive of all brands and labels) to have them properly recycled and receive a coupon for money off their next H&M purchase.

2012: Copenhagen hosts the world's largest conference on sustainability and fashion.[58]

2012: Eco-fashion designer Titania Inglis wins the 2012 Ecco Domani Fashion Foundation Award in Sustainable Design and is featured in *Elle* magazine.

January 2012: NYC hosts the first annual local supplier showcase, named "City Source."[59]

February 2012: Meryl Streep wears Lanvin's first ever eco-friendly gown to the Oscars.[60]

April 2012: Luxury group Kering (formally PPR) launches a five-year sustainability improvement plan across its brands.[61]

June 2012: Uniqlo commits to abstaining from using wool from sheep subjected to mulesing.[62]

August 2012: Sustainable Apparel Coalition launches the Higg Index "to evaluate material types, products, facilities, and processes based on a range of environmental and product design choices."[63]

September 2012: The Green Shows are included in the Mercedes Benz Fashion Week at Lincoln Center for the first time and feature a handful of eco-designers in a styled presentation.

September 2012: Eco-brand Chinti & Parker collaborate with Gwyneth Paltrow to create a limited-edition clothing line available at Goop.com.[64]

October 2012: Levi's launches Waste<Less collection featuring jeans made from recycled plastic bottles.[65]

October 2012: The Soil Association and the Global Organic Textile Standard (GOTS) launch a global organic cotton campaign, Have You Cottoned On Yet? It's the largest campaign of its kind.[66]

November 2012: Greenpeace International publishes *Toxic Threads*, which investigates the use of toxic chemicals in the production of leading brands' clothing. In the following months many of these brands commit to detoxing their supply chains.[67]

February 2013: H&M launches in-store textile recycling program for customers.[68]

As you can see, year by year eco-fashion has gained ground. Not only are small upstarts and emerging designers making ethical and environmental efforts, but major fashion retailers and the media are taking on the tasks as well. This is not a trend or even a movement; this is a reboot, and you are a part of it.

Now it's your turn. This book will give you the tools and resources to align your values with your personal style. Going forward, you will be educated and confident in every purchase you make. Your purchases will send a clear message to retailers about the kinds of responsible and ethical clothing options you expect in the twenty-first century. In doing so, you will play your part in this fashion rebirth and help change the world.

CHAPTER 2

THE INTEGRITY INDEX

"Let integrity fashion your character in all walks of life. As it will shape the person you will become."

—SIMONE DACOSTA

Buying clothes is not that different from buying groceries. We want what we are purchasing to be of the highest quality, good for us, and good for the planet. We want it to be grown and managed responsibly so that it can help us look and feel our best without doing damage to the environment or other human beings in the process.

Let's assume that your standards for taste are already the highest. When you're choosing apples, for instance, you might also like to know whether they were grown locally, pesticide-free, non-GMO, linked to supporting a group of people or co-op, or simply in season. Those considerations, along with the delicious taste and the fragrance of the apple, play a role in your final decision to make a purchase.

This is, in practice, considered shopping, and it applies to how you purchase clothing as well. The first step toward building a wardrobe that is stylish and sustainable is understanding the playing field. What are the issues? What areas deserve your focus and attention? By getting to know the alternatives and the emerging technologies, you'll be better prepared to make streamlined, accurate decisions before you even walk into the fitting room.

There are sixteen ways of looking at any garment, from how it's dyed, to what it's made of, to who made it. These sixteen factors make up what I call the Integrity Index. As you familiarize yourself with the issues of garment production, the Integrity Index will help you identify those issues that really get to you and the ones you'd like to get behind.

As you become more acquainted with the criteria for fair fashion, you're going to find that many of the factors that make up considered fashion are not very different from foodstuffs, particularly when it comes to natural fibers, many of which begin their lives as a crop in a field on a farm.

LABEL LOGIC

Just as you might look on the back or side of a food carton to review the ingredients, you can look at a hang tag (attached to the outside of the garment) or the inside tag (usually along the back neckline or inside right seam) to discover what the garment is made from, where it was made, and how best to care for it. Sometimes the information found on the tag is enough to make a purchase confidently, and other times you may need to dig deeper and visit the brand's website to learn about their manufacturing practices and Corporate Social Responsibility (CSR) initiatives.

This label comes from Pickwick & Weller, a basics brand out of Los Angeles that focuses on vertical integration production in California (vertical integration means that everything, from design creation to manufacturing to distribution, is done in one localized place). Straight off the tag from the inside seam of one of their T-shirts, I was able to see that they produce locally (in the United States) and that they use a sustainable fiber called Tencel. Those two pieces of information, coupled with my positive response to the cut and style of the T-shirt, were sufficient in helping me navigate my sartorialist's dilemma; I was able to align my values with my style without compromise. Boom!

When you pick up a garment, what qualifications do you use to think about it? Do you think about color? Texture? Whether you can wash it in the machine or have to take it to the dry cleaner? Then you're already familiar with some of the factors you're about to encounter on the next few pages. The kind of dyes used to color a textile or natural versus synthetic fabric composition—like a cotton T-shirt that can be line dried or a poly blend jacket that must be taken to the dry cleaners—are all part of the sixteen ways of looking at any garment.

The Integrity Index will help you identify the simple questions that you can ask about every garment, such as: Is it natural? Is it grown organically and without pesticides? How does it support or harm groups of people who live near the areas where the fibers are dyed and turned into fabric? Did the dyes originate as crops themselves or were they cooked up in a lab?

By the end of this section you'll understand the environmental impact of that upcycled polyester shirt that used to be a bunch of used water bottles and the hand-sewn modal shift dress that was dyed with vegetable dyes at the mill down the road. You'll know how organic cotton and conventional cotton are grown. You'll see the difference between recycling, up-cycling, and down-cycling. And you'll be a smarter, more competent consumer everywhere you go.

In this chapter you'll begin to self-select standards to set up your Diamond Diagram (revealed in the next chapter) so you can shop anywhere, anytime with confidence, awareness, and ease! Here's how:

First, read through the following sixteen items. As you read, highlight the factors that really speak to you. Choose four to five criteria that you care about the most. The bottom line of considered fashion is that the choices you make at the register and at the keyboard—at sample sales, at boutiques, at pop-up shops and department stores—send messages to manufacturers and designers about what matters to you. And the more you know, the more YOU can be involved in saving the planet and protecting workers.

This is a pretty comprehensive chapter (that is my disclaimer), so if you already know which environmental or ethical initiatives are a priority for you, you can flip forward to find them in the pages ahead for a little refresher. If you are unsure about which issues are most important to you—let alone those that exist in the fashion space—reading thoroughly through this chapter is essential. What follows is the Sweet Sixteen of the Integrity Index.

1. Natural and Low-Impact Dyeing: What Color Is It?

Color is transformative: the bright red shirt you just bought can lift your mood, complement your skin tone, and set you apart from the crowd. Unfortunately, if you picked it up at Old Navy for $10, it was probably colored through a normal dye process. With a standard dyeing process, fibers are prepped for dyeing with bleach and coated with chemicals so that dye remains intact on the finished products to give them their vibrant color. The process off-gasses nitrogen and sulphur dioxides, chemicals that can wreak havoc on the environment when released into water systems.

....

ECO-INSIGHT—WHAT IS OFF-GASSING?

As materials and products are exposed to oxygen, they can release noxious gases that are harmful to the environment and living organisms around them. When these chemicals are released into the air, water, or soil around us, it is called off-gassing.

In the United States, the Environmental Protection Agency (EPA) and other environmental regulatory bodies have issued production standards that require removal of pollutants before being expelled into waterways and the use of filters to protect air-quality output. That's good news for us here in the States, but it's no secret that much of the world's textile production is now taking place in Asia, where standards are not as diligently established or enforced. Eco-journalist Lucy Siegle found that in developing countries 90 percent of all wastewater is dumped directly into streams and rivers without treatment. People who live near the mills that produced your favorite cheap and chic clothes are thus exposed to contaminated water that may produce a laundry list of health risks.

....

Why You Should Care

Today, there are more than ten thousand dyes with a synthetic origin commercially available, and experts estimate that 12 to 15 percent of these toxic dyes are emitted as liquid waste or sewage during the dyeing and finishing processes.[1] The consequences are significant. These effluents greatly disrupt our ecosystems, pollute our water streams, leach chemicals into our soil, cause skin irritations, and, more seriously, have carcinogenic implications. Want cancer? I didn't think so!

DYE JOB—HOW TO TELL IF IT WAS NATURAL OR CHEMICAL

Bluesign is a third-party supply-chain assessor that looks at both the chemical input and output of textile production processes (specifically dyeing) and holds manufacturers accountable to higher standards in accordance with the following five principles: resource productivity, consumer safety, air emissions, water emissions, and occupational health and safety.

Although dyes are not commonly included on the label, more and more brands are adapting the transparency policy of listing the dyes or methods they use, especially if they are natural or low impact. One of the best labeling standards out there is the bluesign seal of approval. Brands boasting a blue-sign are practicing low-impact or natural dyeing processes that are significantly better for the planet and people who come into contact with them.

Unfortunately, at the moment dye labeling is a little like acing a test. When you do well, you proudly share your results, and if you didn't do so well, you keep it to yourself. That is what is happening in the dye world. So keep your eye out for brands that are openly sharing their good dye practices, and know that you can pretty safely assume that those who are not are still using very toxic and chemically intensive dyes they don't want to talk about.

Natural Dyes

Unlike their destructive chemically based cousins, natural dyes are grown or extracted from plants, animals, and minerals that occur in the natural world. Although natural dyes are the most "natural" option, they still have a downside: it's easy to get color out of flowers like hibiscus, but it's tough to get them to stick to fibers. This means that most natural dyes require a bonding agent, or mordant, to fix color to fabrics. Because common mordants are chemically based or contain heavy metals like chromium and copper, even natural dyes come with a disclaimer. Another downside is that natural dyes must be applied in greater amounts than their toxic relatives in order to get a real pop of color, so using them uses more water in the process.

Bottom line: natural dyes are still natural and are significantly less toxic than normal chemical dyes, even though they are usually more water intensive. Luckily, new technologies continue to develop nontoxic mordants that can aid natural dyeing, and natural dyeing may indisputably lead the way in sustainable practices for the future of textile dyeing.

Brand Blurb: Christoph Frehsee, cofounder of Amour Vert

Amour Vert is a contemporary women's wear line that focuses on domestically made garments from environmentally conscious and sustainable fabrics as well as low-impact dyeing processes. (Check out AmourVert.com)

"I've heard that 20–25 percent of the environmental impact from the textile and fashion industry is caused by dyeing processes. What is really shocking is that the off-cuts from cut and sew production are considered and treated as toxic waste, and that is because of the dyes used. So you have to ask yourself, if the manufacturers are required to treat this excess material as toxic waste, but yet are allowed to use the same material to produce the clothing we buy and put next to our skin—isn't something wrong here?!"

Christoph and his team at Amour Vert raise a very good question, and it is reassuring to learn about brands that are looking at the toxicity of dyeing and finding better ways to meet their end goals. The brand Prophetik is a great example of a high-fashion brand that uses nontoxic natural dyes to create amazing hues for their collections; they're especially known for using indigo to produce vibrant blues. Designer Sasha Duerr gets major props for taking natural dyeing a step further by coloring yarn with food waste that doesn't require a toxic mordant. She uses onion skins, turmeric, coffee grounds, pomegranates, and blackberries to offer a cornucopia of colors that give chemically derived hues a run for their money without the toxic byproducts of normal dye processes.

Low-Impact Dyes

Low-impact dyes are synthetic dyes that may or may not be petroleum based and require less water to process than natural dyes. They can be used in a closed-loop production cycle, which means the discarded dye present after the dyeing process can be cycled back into use. Low-impact dyes offer greater color options than natural dyes, often do not require a chemical mordant or heavy metals during processing, and have a higher absorption level than natural dyes (70 to 80 percent higher). Generally they do not contain mordants or toxic chemicals, and this allows them to be classified as eco-friendly by the Oeko-Tex Standard 100 international certification, an independent testing and certification system for textiles.

At the moment low-impact dyeing is both the more popular and mainstream method for tempering the cost of textile dyeing from an environmental and resource standpoint. It is very popular in the fashion industry, and certain brands have adopted low-impact dyes as part of their supply-chain production.

As you can see, textile dyeing is anything but black and white. There are trade-offs for each method. In general I am in support of the low-impact dyeing process as the leading method. Although natural dyes are not synthetic, they are also not low impact. Low-impact dyeing is a step in the right direction, with a foothold in mass production that is certain to become cleaner as technologies evolve.

Brand Blurb: Spotlight on Alternative Earth by Alternative Apparel

Alternative Apparel is a clothing company that has made responsibly made basics their business. (Check out AlternativeApparel.com)

"We use low-impact dyes for everything in our Alternative Earth line. This means that they do not contain any heavy metals or toxic substances, nor are they petro-chemically based. The absorption (or fixation) rate for these dyes averages 75%, which means we are able to use less dye to produce our color and less water to rinse them in the process. We also use low-impact dyes in many of the products outside of the Alternative Earth line."

2. Natural Fibers: What's It Made Of?

Fiber is the basic building block of fashion and thus has become a leading factor that many designers consider before they even get to the design phase. Natural fibers include naturally occurring plant and animal fibers, like cotton, organic cotton, silk, and leather, and they are produced with or without pesticides and other chemicals. They can also include bioengineered fibers like corn and milk protein fibers.

GETTING TO KNOW NATURAL FIBERS

Fiber	Pesticides/ Chemicals	Water Use	Biodegradable	Recyclable
cotton	yes	high	yes	yes
organic cotton	no	high	yes	yes
flax	no	high	yes	yes
bamboo	yes	low	yes	yes
hemp	not always	low/med	yes	yes
nettle	not always	low/med	yes	yes
ramie	not always	low/med	yes	yes
jute	no	low/med	yes	yes
modal (beech wood pulp)	yes	med	yes	yes
silk	no	low/med	yes	yes
leather	not always	med/high	yes	yes
soy	not always	med/high	yes	yes
corn (PLA)	yes	med/high	yes	yes
milk/protein	yes	med	yes	yes

Natural fibers are biodegradable, so over time exposure to air, sunlight, and water will break them down into simpler substances. That's a huge plus for supporting their use. A number of them, like cotton and bamboo, are also recyclable, so they can either be shredded back to their fiber state and respun into a repurposed yarn (typically with added virgin fiber for strength) and woven or knitted into a new fabric, or they can be down-cycled into something else (like stuffing for a dog bed or insulation).

The downside to natural fibers is that they often are very thirsty. All said and done, the average conventional cotton T-shirt requires around seven hundred gallons of water (that's equal to twenty-two bathtubs!) to produce. However, production of the same T-shirt using organic, fair trade farming reduces that number by 60 percent. If this sounds like the T for you, just look for a certified organic cotton T-shirt from brands like American Apparel, Stewart+Brown, or Stateside.

The trade-off for producing fabrics that are biodegradable and not synthetically made from petroleum or other toxic chemical processes (like those used to make rayon or viscose) allows them to stay high on the chart as an eco-friendly choice.

ECO-INSIGHT—TOXIC CLOTHING COCKTAILS

There are six synthetic fibers to avoid:
nylon, rayon, polyester, acetate, acrylic, spandex.

Synthetic fibers are the opposite of natural fibers. They are like carefully mixed cocktails, incorporating the use of various chemicals in specific ratios to achieve a desired anticolor-fade property or no-iron effect. Yet their convenient characteristics come with a heavy dose of perflourinated chemicals (PFCs). According to the EPA, PFCs have been classified as cancer-causing compounds. Not only are researchers finding that these PFCs may leach into ground water, air, and soil during production but they may also be absorbed or inhaled directly. That is why they recommend consumers wash new synthetic-based clothing at least three times before wear. However, no amount of washing will release that chemical concoction because it is their job to stay put and serve their purpose (guard against static, stay wrinkle-free, remain electric green, etc.) time and time again.

Why You Should Care

On average, synthetic fibers take anywhere from two hundred to four hundred years to biodegrade, off-gassing along the way, and this contributes to major shifts in our natural atmospheric balance. Following climate change talks in Copenhagen in December 2009, off-gassing (also referred to as outgassing) was listed as "one of the dangerous anthropogenic warming effects that the Copenhagen summit is trying to head off."[2] In other words, synthetic textile waste that is sitting in landfills trying its hardest to biodegrade is releasing carbon and other gasses into the atmosphere and undermining our very efforts to keep global temperatures from reaching an overall disastrous increase of two degrees Celsius worldwide, which scientists report as an ominous shift into a "dangerous climate" changing too quickly for ecosystems to adapt.

Brand Blurb: David Peck, founder of David Peck CROP,

David Peck shares his advice for consumers who are ready to take steps to wear no evil and embrace style with sustainability. (Check out DavidPeckCollection.com)

"I think that any discussion of sustainability has to start with quality and design. If products are not made to last in both of these areas, then you start to neutralize any other factors that might be sustainable about the garment. I would encourage consumers who are interested in sustainability to educate themselves on what truly well-made garments look like. Well-made clothes also fit better, and that in turn, makes you feel better. When you feel great about what you are wearing you tend to use it more often and keep it longer. That, in and of itself, is a huge step toward sustainability."

Virtuous Synthetics

The main argument for using natural fibers is that they have existed in nature for centuries, and at the end of their lifecycle they biodegrade back into the earth and support the ecosystem as a whole. Humans have tried to outdo nature by creating materials in the lab, and some of these synthetic materials, while unnatural, can stand the test of time and are reusable in a more immediate way than natural fibers. But that reusability has a cost.

Here's an example: plastic PET bottles that have lived out their usefulness as water porters can grow up to be recycled into polyester yarn and used to produce clothing. If the garments are made with 100 percent PET, they can be recycled again into yarn for another round of producing textiles at the end of their lifecycle.

All of that sounds really sustainable, but here's the catch: we're still talking about plastic. And although plastic might hold its own in lifecycles, its blessing is also its downfall: it doesn't biodegrade. This discussion is a bit of a catch-22. Is it better to use synthetic fibers that hold up over time or natural ones whose lifecycles are not as long but biodegrade? That's where you have to make your own personal call. I'm all for multiple lifecycles, but ultimately I'd rather see a product embrace infinite lifecycles by remaining pure enough to go back into the earth and contribute to a greater, closed-loop system. If you must buy a synthetic, given its leading role as a recyclable textile, pure polyester is the best choice.

If you're not ready to give up your spandex leggings or nylon swimsuit, don't worry. Advancements in the industry are offering more choices. A new type of polyester made from polylactic acid (from corn), known as PLA, is synthetically made from a natural fiber that does biodegrade. This development of biopolymers made from plant-based materials rather than those found in fossil fuels hold promise for the future of eco-fashion.

3. Organic: How Is It Grown?

The simplest definition of organic means that the product—in this case, using raw materials to produce fabric like cotton, bamboo, or hemp—doesn't utilize any pesticides or fertilizers. Buying clothes from our favorite brands that support organic fabric production helps to ensure that our planet's soil and water won't be poisoned with pesticides.

It takes one-third of a pound of pesticides to grow the cotton for a single conventional T-shirt. Multiply that by the fact that 11 to 12 percent of all agricultural pesticides (and 25 percent of all insecticides) used globally are meant for growing conventional cotton, and that basic T-shirt no longer looks like a harmless souvenir. As these chemicals seep into our water supply, the repercussions keep spreading. An estimated 14 million people in the United States across sixteen different states are drinking contaminated water, and the local municipalities are not removing the carcinogenic waste effectively.

How, you may ask, is this possible? Well, it has to do with timing: pesticides leach into ground water slowly over time. The US Geological Survey (under the US Department of the Interior) openly declares that "the effects of past and present land-use practices may take decades to become apparent in ground water." Therefore, when chemical levels from pesticide and fertilizer use are tested in our drinking ground water, accurate levels are not reflected or managed. With 50 percent of the nation's drinking water supply coming from ground water and 95 percent of the population living in agricultural areas relying on clean ground water for drinking, we can easily see how important this issue is.[3]

And that's just how we're hurting our H_2O. Pesticides impact our soil by producing a surface level of salt that sits on the top layer of soil and makes that plot of land virtually unusable for growing anything else. Each year that pesticides are used on a piece of land, the more salinated it becomes. Eventually, it will turn into a biological wasteland.

At the moment using chemicals to grow, process, and finish the materials used to produce apparel are often cheaper than their organic counterparts, but the real costs are deadly. The use of chemicals in the fashion industry has a worldwide effect on natural resources and living organisms. We've seen an increase in the kind of environmental toxicity that contributes to chronic health issues such as carcinogenicity and adverse effects on the immune, endocrine, and other organ systems as well as impaired neurological, reproductive, and developmental systems.

On BioTechArticles.com, industry professionals and PhD students readily share their research on the toxicology of fibers and fabrics used in the textile industry. One microbiology professional stated that "Polyester emits phytoestrogens which act as endocrine disruptors and also promote skin and certain types of cancers. It has been discovered that cancer cells multiply more quickly in polyester test tubes than glass tubes."[4] Scary stuff. And polyester isn't the only toxic culprit. Nylon is known to carry and emit formaldehyde and off-gas greenhouse gasses like nitrous oxide. Viscose and rayon are formed from cellulose wood pulp through a chemically intensive process involving carbon disulphide. As a consequence, carbon disulphide is emitted from these fabrics and shows up as adverse health effects. Those who regularly wear rayon have reported headaches, chest and muscle pain, nausea, vomiting, and insomnia. Although man-made synthetic fibers and chemically fertilized natural fibers may seem like a more accommodating and efficient route in the short term, their long-term costs far outweigh the benefits of using such inorganic processes.

Fortunately, as the industry embraces the use and production of organic materials, the costs will come down and their accessibility will go up. We have already begun to see this change in action. In 2011 H&M was reported as the number-one purchaser of organic cotton. When a big brand makes an investment in their supply chain, the industry shifts. And often those big brands are responding to the consumer's demands (i.e., YOUR demands). Every time you bring a piece of clothing up to the register, you are making a choice. How important is supporting organic production to you?

Brand Blurb:
Anna Singh and Rachel Wood, cofounders of Chinti & Parker

The designing duo behind the classic and eco-luxe label Chinti & Parker share their ideals around creating their label and coining the tagline "Conscious Cloth." (Check out ChintiAndParker.com)

"Conscious cloth is much more than a catchy tagline. It's an ever-present company watchword, reminding us to carefully consider our design choices (fabric, production, style of a garment), and for our shoppers to evaluate their clothing purchases similarly: Do I love this piece? Will it work for me in years to come? Am I okay with where and how it was made?"

For wear-no-evil consumers they suggest, "Keep 'Conscious Cloth' in mind when you're shopping, and assess a garment for its quality, the conditions it's likely to have been made in, whether it suits you, and if it'll fit with your existing wardrobe. Generally, adopt a buy less, but buy better philosophy."

Why You Should Care

Although it may seem that a little exposure to some chemicals here or there won't hurt, the truth is that those chemicals bio-accumulate in our systems as well as those of other living organisms, eventually reaching toxic levels. According to the World Health Organization, around 3 million pesticide poisonings occur each year, which lead to twenty to forty thousand deaths per year.[5]

Supporting organic production has a direct impact on our planet and its natural resources. This also has an impact on us, because we rely on this planet of ours to sustain us. If we don't take care of it, Mother Earth can't take care of us.

4. Fair Trade: Who Makes It?

Fair trade standards ensure that the artisans and farmers who produce the products we consume are compensated at a fair minimum price in a global economy. With the rise of fast fashion, long-term relationships between retailers and fashion manufacturers have diminished and, with them, the accountability for fair wages and standardized safe working conditions. When you purchase a piece that proudly boasts the Fair Trade Standard or World Fair Trade Organization seals, you know you are supporting a supply chain that upholds high standards for the people and processes involved in its production. When brands establish a fair trade supply chain, they create greater transparency and are able to assess that all pieces of their supply chain are acting in accordance with the high environmental and social standards set forth by the World Fair Trade Organization, the World Wildlife Fund (WWF), and the EPA.

EXPERT OPINION: CHRISSIE LAM, FOUNDER OF THE SUPPLY CHANGE

Chrissie Lam is a leading visionary behind mainstream fashion brand partnerships with artisan groups around the world. (Check out TheSupplyChange.org)

"Gone are the days of fair trade fashion being associated with poorly designed 'guilt purchase' goods. Through social impact sourcing, brands can create unique and profitable products with a compelling story and impact behind them—profits with principles. Fair trade fashion is not a fad. It is the future of fashion."

Brand Blurb:
Julie Rubiner, facilitating manager of Knits, EILEEN FISHER

Julie Rubiner helps head up the Peru project at EILEEN FISHER, which operates under the guidance of fair trade standards. She shares their vision, production, and her personal reaction to the project:

"Our organic cotton Peruvian project is a completely traceable project and very dear to my heart. It starts with the farmers, who grow organic cotton, and moves onto the spinners, who turn this luxurious fiber into yarn, and then finally the knitters. Every aspect of the process, including the dyeing and finishing, meets the Global Organic Textile Standard. Born and bred in Peru is an easy way to sum it up."

Julie continues, "As a designer, this project gives me a deeper purpose than just designing beautiful clothes. It layers on a sense of responsibility to this community and I see it as a valuable partnership that drives my creativity. All of this work provides the local community (Arequipa, Peru) with fair trade wages and entrepreneurial opportunities, sustaining families and neighborhoods as well as the environment."

Why You Should Care

A fair trade program is a surefire way to ensure that child labor is not being used. It can create benefits for workers by establishing training opportunities that can lead to advancement as well as the creation of much needed health and education facilities.

5. Recycled and Upcycled: Was It Ever Something Else?

Recycling is both an old and new area of the fashion industry. For centuries clothing was passed down within a family—patched, repaired, and resewn—and many now-identified "eco-brands" employ textile recycling simply by using old and discarded stock to produce their collections at a better price. Additionally, designers gather up and unravel discarded woolen sweaters so they can be knit into a new design. (Reclaimed metal made into new jewelry pieces also falls into this category.)

The newest (and, in my opinion, most exciting) form of textile recycling involves reducing a piece of fabric or product, like an old food tray, down to its fiber state to then spin it into a repurposed yarn that can be used to create a new fabric and garment. This kind of textile recycling is available for both natural fibers and synthetic ones. It can also be done using a mechanical method in which the fabric or product being recycled is mechanically shredded down to the fiber level or through a chemical process in which a chemical solvent breaks down the original fabric or product.

The most common kind of recycled textile currently available is recycled polyester, or PET. Polyester may not biodegrade, but its durability makes it a great candidate for repurposed yarn that can be recycled again and again if it is blended only with other polyester. To identify whether a garment or product is made from a recycled material, simply check the tag or the packaging. The manufacturer or brand will clearly state whether a recycled substance has been used, because they know consumers are looking for this today. If you are shopping online, click on product details to see what it is made from. Again, if a recycled material is used, it will say so.

Brands working with Teijin (a leading recycled fabric factory in Japan), like Patagonia and Nau, are exploring a closed-loop system in which the recycled fabric purchased from Teijin is made with the intent that the same fabric sewn into garments will come back to Teijin and go into their supply chain to produce yet another round of recycled fabric at the end of the garments' lifecycle. It all sounds a little like *Physics of the Future*, but these are things that are happening right now and will likely become more and more common in the fashion industry going forward.

Why You Should Care

Every year in the United States 1.3 million tons of textile waste goes into landfills, and 95 percent of that is recyclable.[6] It is a crying shame.

ECO-INSIGHT—THE UPSIDES TO RECYCLING

Just as the recycling industry has grown up around us and helped us to dispose of paper, plastic, and glass products responsibly, textiles will also become a commodity and valuable raw material in a closed-loop supply chain. The upsides to using a recycled textile are numerous. In a report by EcoGear comparing conventional cotton yarn and recycled cotton yarn, they found that "Bearing in mind that in order to manufacture Recycled Cotton yarn (80 percent cotton, 20 percent polyester), not only is there a savings in chemical products, savings in water consumption, savings in the amount of land used for cultivation which could be put to another agricultural use, but in addition, energy savings is over 17 percent, and in fact it could be said that where Recycled Yarn is used as opposed to fully certified Organic Cotton Yarn, there is even less impact on the environment." Wow.

Upcycled

Upcycled is a term that is growing in recognition and popularity. When something is upcycled, it is made from raw materials that were originally intended to become something else. One example is how luxury handbag label The Sway NYC uses discarded leather scraps from high-quality factories in Italy to produce beautiful leather bags, clutches, and jackets. Another example is TM1985, a brand that has a cool urban aesthetic and uses old army surplus bags to make iPad cases, wallets, and backpacks.

So what is the difference between recycling and upcycling? When you recycle a glass bottle you get another glass bottle. Upcycling requires a little more creativity, as the material is reworked into a new product. Some truly amazing designs and items have emerged from the upcycling process because they pushed the designer to utilize what material they had in front of them rather than employ an endless supply of raw materials.

Upcycling is rightfully staking its claim in the fashion industry, as designers look to their overstock and bolts of leftover fabric to create new garments from fabric that was previously meant and used for something else. It is one of the best ways to decrease landfill textile waste and make use of quality resources already in existence. Zara has actually been a leader in this space due to their short-term production model. They reported producing a red dress in a shape that apparently was not as hot as they had hoped. So they recalled the dresses from their stores in Spain and reworked the same material into a top with a more flattering and fashion-forward shape. The tops were redistributed into the stores, and they sold like hotcakes.

Brand Blurb: The Sway NYC

Belinda Pascal of The Sway NYC tells us how using excess leather from quality-leather factories has led to signature sell-out designs. (Check out TheSwayNYC.com)

"The beauty about the excess is that it comes in such different shapes that we can really create a variety of designs and techniques and keep it unique. The triangle patchwork, for example, is a popular patchwork technique for us. We have different-sized triangles for different pieces. The triangle clutch has been a best seller since day one. It's about using edgy shapes and styling to get the look right. First it's about beauty, form, and function. When we have passed all those tests, and the customer realizes our pieces are recycled they feel it's a bonus and that makes them feel better about buying it!"

Why You Should Care

Upcycling drastically reduces waste and allows for visionary creations that are sometimes more unique and interesting than their standard fast-fashion counterparts.

6. Local: Was It Made Nearby?

The saying "think global, act local" has become a slogan for the twenty-first century. Many independent thinkers have backed away from the industry habit of shipping various pieces of one whole around the world for sourcing, production, finishing, and, finally, sales. These days, as we better understand the costs of a process like this, we recognize that it is not the most effective way of doing things.

Nor is it good for people. Currently, 40 million garment workers toil over our frivolous fashion needs in South America, Africa, Bangladesh, Thailand, Cambodia, India, Vietnam, and, of course, China. The driving factor of going overseas for production is to gain a higher profit margin by cutting costs with cheaper labor and material costs. With this objective leading the way, companies and brands that seek overseas production no longer exercise a commitment to suppliers and manufacturers. They go where the cheapest price exists. There is no loyalty.

Some argue that this expansion into global production yields jobs and opportunities for those involved, but that is an optimistic picture whose reality is a rarity. A more accurate depiction includes unsafe and unethical working conditions for employees, underage workers, sweatshops, unprotected exposure to toxic chemicals, unsupervised environmental depletion of natural resources for the surrounding community, and a constant fear of job loss.

Contrast that with the value of local production. Designing locally reduces the CO_2 emissions of shipping, supports the local economy, and allows greater control over proper production. Going local can also help to ensure multilocal diversity by enlisting the local traditions and materials of a culture. It cuts transportation costs, both environmental and monetary, and supplies local jobs. And local production puts the environmental standards directly under our noses. This closeness allows us to better detect air and water quality and to ensure proper standards are met and enforced.

When startups, smaller designers, and global brands embrace a local initiative, they have the opportunity to incorporate regional materials, skills, and cultural knowledge into the products they offer, thus creating culturally and regionally relevant styles that consumers can celebrate for their authenticity. In addition to fostering value for the people and places of local production, brands diversify their offering to the marketplace and have the potential to create added value to their bottom line. As an example, both American Eagle Outfitters and Kate Spade have, in the past, partnered with a local community to produce jewelry or accessories that apply the local skill set (such as weaving) and also take on the local style aesthetic of that community. These minicollections that they make available in their stores and online bring something different to the table and, therefore, add to a more diversified offering from a mainstream brand.

Brand Blurb: Lauren Podoll, cofounder of The Podolls

The Podolls is a women's wear fashion line rooted in eco-fashion ethos, created by a husband-and-wife team (Josh and Lauren Podoll) and based out of San Francisco, California. (Check out ThePodolls.com)

"When we first started our brand, we were really cognizant of having our products made in the USA. We feel that it not only benefits our community, but that there is an element of satisfaction when you can contact your sewers directly and oversee the production. Even when we did an order for Anthropologie, and we were itty bitty, we were very proud that we stuck with our local production. It felt good to be giving work to these skilled workers, and utilizing the resource of their talent right within the Bay Area."

Why You Should Care

When you support local production, you know you are helping to create long-term relationships, local jobs, economic security for a community, higher and enforced environmental standards, fair wages, safe working conditions, and added value through diversified offerings.

ECO-INSIGHT—ON THE FLIP SIDE

Overseas production is not always bad. Many brands diligently ensure that the suppliers and manufacturers they work with meet their high standards, and in this way they can be viewed as proponents of positive social and economic change. They help teach workers about their rights and can improve their skill levels. The Krochet Kids, ASOS Africa, and People Tree are all examples of this beneficial overseas production model.

7. Social: What Does It Stand For?

Social-linked garments are pieces that come with a cause. Social clothes have benefited charities, women's cooperatives, and disaster-relief funding, so that your cute tote or espadrilles very directly impact a specific group of people. A very mainstream example is FEED bags. Their mission is to eradicate world hunger by selling tote bags with the brand's name and objective clearly printed: FEED. According to FEED's website, hunger and malnutrition kill more people than AIDS, malaria, and tuberculosis combined. For every bag they sell, a donation built into the cost of the bag ensures that a child in Africa has a midday meal at school for a year. TOMS Shoes also falls under this category. The shoes TOMS produces ensure that for every pair sold, another pair is given to a person in need. Donna Karan produces a line called Urban Zen, which links every product to an artisanal group from which the products are made and to which the proceeds go. She has also spearheaded financial relief efforts for Haiti after the catastrophic 7.0 earthquake that struck in 2010 by donating a percentage of the proceeds of purchased garments to organizations actively helping in the area.

Brand Blurb:
Paul van Zyl, Kristy Caylor, and Daniel Lubetzky, cofounders of Maiyet

Maiyet honors and supports artisans in Kenya, Peru, India, and Colombia. The fashion newcomer has quickly gained status as the luxury label to buy for a mix of craftsmanship and contemporary design. They share the basis of their social enterprise model, which is changing the landscape of the fashion industry:

"The beautiful artisanal craft that we've discovered in some of the most unexpected places allows us to celebrate the next generation of global craftsmen. In doing so, we are creating sustainable employment in places that need it most, while also offering the luxury consumer a unique, covetable, beautifully designed product. When our business does well, our artisans thrive, so both of our interests are perfectly aligned.

"Our hope is that the industry follows. We believe the future of fashion is about beautifully handcrafted product made with integrity, authenticity, and transparency. This is the new luxury."

Why You Should Care

Organizations and fashion brands linked to social causes and enterprises are having a profound effect. Lauren Bush's organization FEED has supplied millions of meals to those in need through the sale of the everyday shopping bags and other accessories they offer. Through these organizations, we can make a difference in the lives of others while picking up a stylish piece for our wardrobe.

8. Zero Waste: What Was Left Behind?

As designers and pattern makers push themselves to create patterns for production that utilize most, if not all, the fabric from a cut spool, we have seen an advancement in the fashion industry known as zero waste, or jigsaw puzzle patterning. More and more designers are developing skills in creating patterns and pieces that utilize these methods and reduce the cutting and trimming waste to zero.

....

EXPERT OPINION: TIMO RISSANEN

Timo Rissanen is a professor at Parsons in New York and has been leading the charge around zero-waste theory and application for the past decade. He shares his thoughts on what zero waste means to him:

"Zero-waste fashion design refers to fashion design that ensures that all of the fabric used to make a garment is in the garment. On average, 15 percent of fabric used to make the clothes we wear is wasted during manufacture. All fabric embodies investments of material, water, energy, and labor; recycling fabric waste can only recapture some of these investments. Avoiding waste is always better than recycling it."

....

Why You Should Care

As Timo stated, an estimated 10 to 20 percent of fabric is left on the cutting room floor as waste. That translates to roughly one hundred tons of fabric that is simply wasted each year in the United States alone! From an economics standpoint, that is just bad business. Why would you ever want to allow 20 percent of your materials to go to waste? Let's look at an example: if you were a brand making denim jeans and you did a production run of five thousand pairs, with 20 percent of your raw denim material going to waste, you'd miss out on producing a thousand pairs! As consumers, we get hit with a higher-priced pair of jeans to cover the wasted-materials cost.

9. Slow Fashion: How Much Thought Was Put into It?

Slow fashion is the polar opposite of fast fashion. Think of fast fashion as fast-food chain restaurants. Slow fashion is akin to the locally run and operated restaurants in your neighborhood. The slow movement is based around implementing modes of sustainable fashion development through local sourcing, production, and distribution on a timeline that honors craftsmanship and original designs that embody quality and timelessness. It focuses on alternative paths for creation, production, and distribution of fashion. Thus far, slow fashion is not present in mass-market offerings; its qualities are more attuned to unique and special offerings from smaller design houses or craftspeople.

Brand Blurb: Slow and Steady Wins the Race

Slow and Steady Wins the Race is a New York–based label that stresses low unit production to ensure quality standards and avoid market saturation. They share their involvement in the slow fashion movement:

"Our job as designers really is to provide something thoughtful for the consumer to understand. To understand the benefits of slow fashion—better quality, the justification of certain costs, and the longevity of the item. Good design should not become obsolete."

Why You Should Care

Slow fashion celebrates a return to tradition and local cultural influences, supply, and design, and this means that it is individual instead of derivative. Slow fashion seeks to identify and create pieces that are classic, will not go out of style, and will be steady players in your everyday wardrobe. Fast fashion is so often homogenized and flippant; slow fashion is original, rich, creative, and, of course, timeless.

STYLE SOURCE: SLOW FASHION BRANDS

Elsa & Me	One offering—a classic dress style made to measure in various hues.
Outsider Fashion	Inspired by fashion, made to be worn season after season.
Sctoica	Structured around versatility and timeless designs.
FEIT	Made-to-order shoes for gents.
Slow Palette	Local materials used to create semicouture garments.

STYLE SOURCE: FAST FASHION BRANDS

Forever 21	Popular with the bargain fashion hunters.
Mango*	The safer side of fast fashion. Trendy and office appropriate.
Zara	Fashion influences from Europe made available every week.
Top Shop*	Style straight from the streets of London.
H&M*	Wardrobe building basics infused with über-trendy styles.

*These fast fashion retailers offer eco-conscious lines.

10. Vegan: Is It Animal Friendly?

For many designers, being friendly to the planet extends to being friendly to our companions on Earth. These designers and brands offer vegan fashion pieces that do not use any animal parts in their production. Some have an emotional argument for not using animals in fashion production, and some consider the environmental argument, because the environmental cost of raising and "harvesting" these living beings is significant.

Vegan clothes replace leather and fur with faux versions and extend to another category that is often overlooked in the vegan fashion discussion: silk. Regular silk production kills the silkworms in the process. Look for Peace Silk to ensure that the garment you are purchasing is made without harming the silkworms so they can go on producing more gorgeous fabric for you.

Why You Should Care

Olsen Haus is a leading vegan footwear brand that is resolute in their stance that there is no need to ever harm or use animals in any way for the sake of fashion. They point out that "The livestock/leather industry is the largest contributor to environmental degradation worldwide. It includes massive land deforestation, loss of top soil, contamination of water supply, air pollution, overuse of oil and water, and loss of biodiversity. It produces more greenhouse gases than all the SUVs, cars, trucks, planes, and ships in the world combined, and it is more harmful to the environment than the textile, medicine, fertilizer and paper industries."

LEATHER VS. PLEATHER

I know you all are thinking it, so we might as well have it out and explore the pros and cons of leather versus leather alternatives. This has been a challenging area for me personally, because as I discover new pieces of information, my opinion on this subject keeps changing. It is an important area that deserves our close consideration, surely, and so I offer you the facts and invite you to make your own decision on the topic.

Pleather (plastic leather) is made from PVC, which, you guessed it, doesn't biodegrade and is in fact a chemically rich and energy-demanding fiber to produce. Processing normal leather can be quite toxic too. During the tanning process chrome is used, leaching chromium into our waterways and soil.

If you decide that the real deal is better than faux leather, the best you can do is check that the leather products you purchase come from an organic and humane source that is a byproduct of the meat industry and colored with a vegetable tanning process. The upside to using real leather is that it ages well over time, holds up in the quality sector, and will eventually biodegrade.

Conversely, PVC does not jeopardize an animal's life, cuts down on the environmental costs associated with raising livestock, and can have a very long life itself. The downfall of PVC is that it doesn't age well over time the way leather does, and its production is fairly toxic to the environment, not to mention how it doesn't biodegrade—ever!

At the moment, while the meat industry still exists and we are not a planet full of harmonizing vegans, I am in support of real leather or natural leather alternatives over the faux synthetic leathers. I do consciously try to buy "old" leather as opposed to "new" leather, thus giving it a second lifecycle.

If the choice between leather and plastic is too much, you are in luck! Bia Saldanha is committed to sourcing an Amazonian tree rubber that looks a lot like leather. She has collaborated with Hermes and Veja to produce fashion-forward accessories and footwear that are both ethical and environmentally sound.

11. Water Footprint: How Thirsty Is It?

Recently brands have begun to pay more attention to their water footprint, containing water in a closed system (the hydrological cycle) so that water used for the fashion industry is restricted from use in other areas, like drinking water. Innovation to reduce the waste and pollution of water is essential to the future of fashion—and Mother Earth.

Brand Blurb: Spotlight on Levi's

Levi's is a classic American-heritage clothing company founded by Levi Strauss in 1873, best known for their effortless cool style and signature jeans. (Check out Levi.com)

In an effort to better gauge and control their water footprint, Levi's created a new line of jeans dubbed Water<Less, in which they use a significantly lower level of water to create each pair. According to Levi's, "The average pair of jeans uses 42 liters of water in the finishing process. The Water<Less collection reduces the water consumption by an average of 28% and up to 96% for some new products in the line."

Why You Should Care

The World Economic Forum has declared that we are going to face a water bankruptcy. According to UNEP, within twenty years our water supply demands will increase by 40 percent. Supporting brands that actively lessen their water footprint is a proactive step in the right direction to help ensure that our water supply stays plentiful in the future.

ECO-INSIGHT—GLOBAL TEXTILE INDUSTRY WATER USE

Global textile production currently requires 100 million gallons of water each year.

Let's put that into perspective. On average it takes 20 gallons of water to produce one yard of upholstery weight fabric, like denim. In 2012 the *Wall Street Journal* reported that a classic pair of jeans requires 505 gallons of water. Sure is easy to see how it adds up.

12. Transparency: How Much Are They Telling Me?

As awareness and alternative products become increasingly available, so will the choices we, as consumers, make. To a large extent we are becoming the new social agents of change. It makes sense for brands to embrace movement toward a more transparent and consumer-educating space. The average consumer today is a lot more educated and involved than were shoppers from twenty or even ten years ago. If you're reading this book, you already know that we are voting with our wallets. So don't you deserve an open dialog with a brand about when, where, and how the product you are purchasing was sourced?

Greater transparency from brands like IceBreakers, the IOU Project, and Nike creates the opportunity for a new feedback loop from you, the user. When companies showcase their inner workings and processes, customers can signal support or offer alternative methods, resulting in a collaborative effort aimed at producing the best possible products in the best possible way.

Brand Blurb: Kavita Palmer, founder of the IOU Project

The IOU Project is a brand redefining the fashion space. Founded on the celebration of Indian-made madras fabric and integrating a completely transparent supply chain that consumers can view and also insert themselves into the garment's digitally tracked lifecycle, IOU is leading the future of fashion. (Check out iouproject.com)

"We at IOU believe that true transparency is fundamental to foster responsible consumption—to build back the emotional connection between those who make and we who consume; to de-commoditize product; to empower and engage both the artisan and the consumer by connecting them. Once you know the person who made your product, your relationship with it changes and you are much more engaged with their reality. Awareness of each other is the first step toward mutual respect and collaborative conservation—things we desperately need."

Why You Should Care

Transparency puts brands on the grandstand to display their supply-chain system and offers us the opportunity to better understand whether we support or oppose their methods.

13. Cradle to Cradle: What Happens When I'm Done with It?

Since the Industrial Revolution began, production has been marching to the beat of mass output. It relies on synthetic materials and environmentally degrading manufacturing techniques as well as the assumption that our resources are infinite. That is a terribly flawed assumption to make because it is simply not true.

William McDonough and Michael Braungart, authors of *Cradle to Cradle,* are essentially the forefathers of closed-loop thinking. They propose a new way of designing apparel, one that is part of the twenty-first century instead of the nineteenth century, one that utilizes a cradle-to-cradle design system instead of the cradle-to-grave system by which the majority of today's goods are produced.

With a cradle-to-grave approach, a product is conceptualized, produced, and used, and then at the end of its lifecycle, it winds up in a landfill. Usually the product has been manufactured with nonbiodegradable materials.

A cradle-to-cradle design system accounts for the birth of a product, its use during its lifecycle, and, most importantly, how it will be recycled after its first lifecycle is complete. In order for this process to be successful, a well-thought-out plan must be formulated in the design phase when the product is seen for what it will be in both the immediate and the remote future.

Brand Blurb: Spotlight on Patagonia

Patagonia is a brand that for many is the benchmark for considered production. Their commitment to form, function, and the environment is quite simply their *raison d'être*. (Check out Patagonia.com)

In a concerted effort to close the loop, Patagonia proudly launched their Common Threads initiative to take back used and worn-out Patagonia Capilene to turn it around and have it made into a usable fabric once again. They ran the numbers to make sure their closed-loop efforts were sustainable, finding that the energy saved from recycling used textiles into new yarns and fabric saved 72 percent of the energy used to produce virgin fibers.

Why You Should Care

McDonough and Braungart tell us: "Consider this: all the ants on the planet, taken together, have a biomass greater than that of humans. Ants have been incredibly industrious for millions of years. Yet their productiveness nourishes plants, animals, and soil. Human industry has been in full swing for a little over a century, yet it has brought about a decline in almost every ecosystem on the planet. Nature doesn't have a design problem. People do."

14. Convertible: What Else Can It Do?

Convertible fashion conjures up images from *Clueless,* in which Cher's left-out friend, Tai, awkwardly stands on the sidelines of a school dance and fashions her shirt into multiple looks as an outlet for her anxious boredom. Luckily, you don't need an awkward situation to take advantage of a convertible fashion piece. In fact, many carry-on-only jet-setters regularly use pieces that can be worn in various ways to take them from day to night in sixty seconds. These proverbial fashion stars are carefully constructed to offer reversibility, multiple color ways, and versatile styling options.

Convertible fashion isn't reserved just for apparel, either. A new brand called Eponymous has launched classic handbag shapes with changeable side panels in luxury fabrics and leathers. Celebrities like Kristin Cavallari have been rocking convertible bags for years. In 2010 Kristin was famously photographed strolling the streets of Beverly Hills with the Foley+Corinna Disco City Convertible Bag structured as a day shopper. Later she converted the bag into a smaller, folded-over evening bag for her night out.

Brand Blurb: Jia Li, founder and creative director of Jia Collection

Jia is a collection of versatile fashion created for the woman on the go. Each piece in Jia Collection can be transformed to different looks, thus making dressing for a modern, busy life much easier. Jia shares why she created a convertible label and how it is considered eco. (Check out JiaCollection.com)

"I wanted to make dressing for the modern woman easier. Life for metropolitan working women can get quite demanding. They have to juggle between many tasks and roles that they are trying to fit in, and looking good in all of them is not easy. They have to look appropriate in different places: work, an after-work cocktail party, art openings, charity events, girlfriends get-togethers, etc. By giving women more options in each Jia Collection piece they own, we make getting dressed and looking good a lot easier.

"Convertible fashion provides more utility given the same amount of material used, thereby reducing the material wastage. Convertible fashion also makes it conducive to having much smaller and more edited wardrobes. As a result, we need less storage, smaller living units; there's less laundry to do and more money in the bank."

Why You Should Care

Everyone loves a two-for-one. Whether or not your shopping budget is tight, convertible fashion gives you more styling options than your basic blazer as well as more wiggle room in your suitcase, which makes them the perfect choice for frequent fliers.

15. Secondhand: Who Else Wore It?

Less than a decade ago secondhand shopping carried a taboo connotation by middle- to upper-class shoppers. Today, with Julia Roberts strutting down the red carpet in a vintage Valentino gown, friends getting together to host clothes-swapping parties, and fashion bloggers selling their prized closets online, it has become a mainstream norm.

Clothing can have nine lives thanks to Goodwill and charity shop donations, secondhand consignment shops, designer resale stores, websites, apps, and, of course, the luxury vintage circuit. Since 2001 Goodwill Industries has reported an increase of 67 percent in the sale of donated items, the majority of which are clothing.[7] Today secondhand shopping is booming, and you can conveniently browse and shop on your smart phone with the popular app Poshmark. Online secondhand shopping is also hitting a high, and it can be indulged on various platforms, such as eBay, Threadflip, Copious, Etsy, reFashioner, and Material Wrld, where users can directly engage in listing their own closets online to sell or swap with other users.

That's a good thing, because on average we Americans each throw out sixty-eight pounds of clothing every year. That adds up to 23.8 billion pounds of clothing that winds up in the US landfills alone.[8] The trends and seasons have sped up with the advent of fast fashion, and as a consumer it is hard to keep up without cycling through the fashions ourselves. Yet we all know this can be quite costly, both on our budgets and the planet. And at some point the price for producing fast-fashion goods will bottom out, landfills will reach their capacity, and our natural resources will be exhausted.

Brand Blurb: Cheryl Campbell, managing director of the Eileen Fisher Community Foundation on the Eileen Fisher GREEN EILEEN Initiative

In April of 2013 Eileen Fisher stores across the United States opened their doors to take back your used and gently worn Eileen Fisher pieces. These pieces are then sorted, and ones that meet a good condition standard are placed in a Green Eileen store, where customers can shop used Eileen Fisher clothing at a discount. (Check out GreenEileen.org)

"Eileen kept hearing that customers felt sad parting with their garments because they were in really good shape. When they learned about the GREEN EILEEN concept, it made it easier to donate their clothing to support a good cause. Initially we had a handful of stores that accepted garments. Now, customers can recycle clothes at all sixty EILEEN FISHER stores across the country. To date, we've collected over 100,000 garments and raised over $1.5 million for an organization that supports women and girls."

Secondhand cycling is one of the best ways to participate in sustainable fashion. Nothing is more effective in saving our resources than reusing what already exists.

16. Style: How Sweet Is It?

A few years back the über-chic duo behind WhoWhatWear.com and coauthors of the *Who What Wear* books, Hillary Kerr and Catherine Power, hosted a book signing in New York City's fashion alley, Soho. As a huge fan of their work—style advice via celebrity outfit breakdowns—I was thrilled when they made time to chat with me after signing my copy of their first book. As they stood before me, looking effortlessly chic, we chatted away, and they offered their take on the importance of style.

Simply put, they said, there are two groups that people fall into: a) fashion devotees and b) fashion detractors. The devotees revel in creating outfits that incorporate new trends and either a learned or intuitive knowledge around mixing textures, patterns, colors, and proportions. They find fashion a necessary outlet for their budding or established self-expression. (Hint: if you are reading this book, you're in group A.) The detractors, however, view fashion as a puzzling distraction, a waste of time, and an indulgence fit only for the vain. Of course, they are entitled to their opinions. Yet the fact remains that everywhere we go, in every situation, and with every outfit or look we put forward, we are judged. So why not make sure people are judging your best self?

Ever heard of enclothed cognition? Simply put, it is a theory detailing the effects that clothing has on our cognitive processes. Professor Adam D. Galinsky published a study in the *Journal of Experimental Social Psychology*, and it states that "clothes invade the body and brain, putting the wearer into a different psychological state." If reason follows, it is fair to say that just as you are what you eat, you are also what you wear. I am sure we can all relate to pulling together the perfect outfit and stepping out the door feeling like a million bucks. That's because our personal style and how we present ourselves to the world through our dress creates identity and allows us to indulge in new ones.

It pretty much goes without saying that if all or any of the previously mentioned Integrity Index items were present in a garment but there was no sign of design or style, the piece would fall flat. Actually, you would be stuck back at the beginning, feeling the frustration of the sartorialist's dilemma—attempting to align one's style with one's values. If we are to put in place all of the other items from the Integrity Index while neglecting style, the entire system would break down. Let me give you an example: I was meeting a friend for a drink in London, a woman who was known for both her style and her commitment to ethical fashion. When I walked into the swanky bar where we had agreed to meet, she was easy to spot—but no longer because of her killer style. Her outfit was a hodgepodge of three colors that had become a stringent guideline for her wardrobe, and none of the pieces quite complemented the others. She was still the lovely bright-eyed and beautiful woman I knew her to be, but something felt off. She had been so stylish, but now her style felt confused and less than chic.

She explained to me that her way of demonstrating sustainable fashion in action was to purchase a limited number of pieces each year and then mix and match those pieces all year long. Although her logic and practice were in fact very sustainable, her technique fell short on the stylish side of things. She was letting her rules run her life and had lost the creative stylish spark she had when I first met her years before. This book was created to help show you that you needn't let your values run your style.

In fact, this is a book specifically about aligning fashion to your values without sacrificing personal style, and, therefore, we absolutely have to take aesthetics into account. The goal is to find pieces that legitimately resonate on both levels. So, you guessed it, the final factor, the one that is nonnegotiable, is style.

Why You Should Care

If a piece of fashion is produced in a more sustainable or ethical way but falls short on the fashion front, it cannot be a real contender as a wardrobe builder.

YOUR INTEGRITY, YOUR INDEX

When we're trying to learn new things and change our habits, the biggest mistake we can make is trying to do everything at once. When it comes to sustainable fashion, I learned that the hard way! I first identified the sixteen items that make up the Integrity Index when I was a grad student who was eating, sleeping, and breathing all things related to sustainability in fashion, and so I immediately attempted to follow all of them at once. Unfortunately, my sustainability was not sustainable. I found out pretty quickly that seeking to uphold all sixteen factors at the same time for any single piece of fashion was downright impossible. Gradually I worked out a system that allowed for real-life application, flexibility, and style success, and in the next chapter I'm going to share that system with you. For now let's review what caught your attention most while you were reading through the Integrity Index.

Natural/Low-Impact Dyes	Natural Fibers	Organic	Fair Trade
Recycled/Upcycled	Secondhand	Local	Social
Zero Waste	Convertible	Vegan	Low Water Footprint
Transparent	Cradle to Cradle	Slow Fashion	Style

Which of the sixteen items on the list really resonated? I'd like you to circle the four or five that made your moral compass spin. Identifying these initiatives is the first part of the *Wear No Evil* system. You'll come back to them in the next chapter (where we put them into action). For now, take a deep breath and congratulate yourself: you've read the playbook.

Now you're ready to play.

CHAPTER 3

THE DIAMOND LIFE

"Know first who you are; then adorn yourself accordingly."

—EPICTETUS

This chapter, coupled with the last, is what you have been looking for as a conscious cool hunter. It is the key to shopping for style and sustainability without sacrifice or an overload of unmanageable information. In the previous chapter you learned about all the ways a piece of fashion can be considered less evil, better, or positively good. Then you were asked to single out the factors that you support most. That was the heavy lifting in this book and the first part of the *Wear No Evil* method. The Diamond Diagram is the second part of that equation.

INTEGRITY INDEX + DIAMOND DIAGRAM = THE *WEAR NO EVIL* SYSTEM

The Diamond Diagram is all about creating a framework, one that is simple and flexible. It is based on a classic mathematical shape—the diamond. My high school PE teacher would be proud, because learning how to use the diamond shape to your advantage here is best done by relating it to baseball.

As you may have guessed, the Diamond Diagram has four corners: home base (at the bottom), first base (to the right), second base (at the top), and third base (out to the left). For each of the bases (including home) a slot is open for an Integrity Index factor to occupy. Essentially, there are four open spaces to fill in, and home base is where you start. Whereas the other bases are flexible and open for the Integrity Index factor of your choice, home base is reserved for style. This makes sense, because as we've previously discussed, without style, there wouldn't be a game.

To fill the bases, you need only four factors, but I like to have an extra one on the bench, waiting to play. So before we go any further, take a moment to jot down your top four Integrity Index Factors, besides style, here:

1. Style
2.
3.
4.
5.

With five clearly defined factors we are ready to move forward. Let's use my preferred Integrity Index factors to see how this works.

My list looks like this:

1. Style
2. Natural fibers
3. Organic
4. Local production
5. Socially linked products

Every time I fill a base I get closer to wearing less evil. The addition of my selected standards for each piece is applied in a limited and realistic way. For instance, if I filled home base with style and then added organic to get to first base, that would be a great step toward sustainability, and two out of the four bases would be filled. The goal is to try to fill all four bases for as many products (or purchases) as possible. That said, I realize that filling all four all of the time is still a challenge. That is why this model is flexible. Filling four out of four is awesome, but so is three or two out of four. The only rule to making this system work is that you can't dip below two fillers. That means you can't buy something just because it is cool. It has to have integrity creds to back up its style status.

Let me give you an example: I bought a T-shirt from Everlane that helped to update my wardrobe. It had style, was made of cotton (a natural fiber), and I know that Everlane proudly makes their clothing in Los Angeles, California. One, two, three—check!

Here's another example: often when I am traveling I will dip into boutiques to see what they have on the racks and pick up a piece or two to add to my wardrobe. Again, I will only pick it out if it is stylish and catches my eye. Then I look at the tag on the inside of the garment to see whether it is made from natural fibers (say, a modal and cotton blend) and made in the country I am visiting. If so, it is a go.

Starting to make sense? One more piece of information that will make using the Diamond Diagram even easier is to think of the open bases as musical chairs. They don't require the same integrity factor each time or need to be in any order. In a sense you can think of all your integrity factors as players patiently waiting on the bench, ready to be put into action at any time. When style occupies home base I have four other factors and three bases to play with for any given purchase. Say I am at a fundraiser party and have the opportunity to support the cause by purchasing a T-shirt. That purchase would fill two bases (home, considering I find the shirt stylish and something I would wear plus first base, which would be occupied by my social factor). Yet if I were looking to purchase a T-shirt and wasn't at a fundraiser but instead a mainstream boutique, I might find one made from 100 percent modal. That too would be a double hitter, because both style and natural fibers would occupy home base and first, respectively.

By narrowing your integrity factors to five (including style), you can easily navigate this model and create confidence in ethical shopping anywhere you go.

Got a grasp on that? Good. Once you get comfortable with manipulating the Diamond Diagram and inserting your integrity factors in various combinations, we can further simplify the system by assigning levels.

SHADES OF GREEN

The Diamond Diagram gives you four bases to fill and three levels to attain. We've already established that style alone isn't enough to warrant a purchase in the wear-no-evil world we are creating. To step onto level one you'll need to fill two bases. Level two requires three filled bases, and level three demands all four to be occupied.

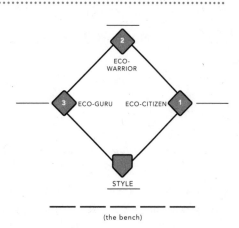

Level One (First Base): Eco-Citizen

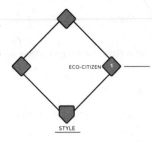

Home: Style

1st Base:

In my mind a citizen is a person who is aware of their surroundings and community and actively plays a part in creating the environment they wish to experience. As an eco-citizen, you are educated and aware and ready to play a part in shaping the world around you, even if it is simply by taking one considered fashion factor and upholding its value and impact. When I operate at this level my motto is "some is better than none," and I know that is the truth. The eco-citizen slot is a great starting point when shopping with your values in mind.

To be an eco-citizen you must fill home and first base before making a purchase. So revisit your top four considered fashion factors and plug them in here. Let's use mine as an example. Remember that my top five factors are: style, natural fibers, organic, local, and social. To be an eco-citizen I would need to satisfy the non-negotiable style factor plus one other factor before making a purchase.

Say I purchase a pair of Warby Parker sunglasses. They aren't made from natural material, nor are they organic or made locally, but they are linked to a social cause and quite stylish. Thus, I've filled two bases—home (style) and first (social). Perfect. As an eco-citizen, my goal is to check off two bases, which is definitely better than none! The important thing to remember is the four considered fashion factors you've chosen to support. You can move them in and out of this eco-citizen arrangement as you please and as they come up while you are shopping.

I hope you can see the flexibility that exists by using this system. As long as you have the groundwork in place, you can confidently shop the world as a global eco-citizen.

Level Two (Second Base): Eco-Warrior

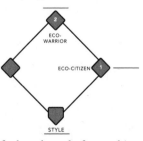

Home: Style

1st Base:

2nd Base:

When you move into the eco-warrior position you satisfy three bases before making a purchase. This is the level at which I typically operate at, and I am very happy to report that it is easier than you think. You can probably see where this is going (it is quite simple!), but let me give you the lowdown on level two.

The best way for me to explain the eco-warrior level is to do so with an example. So let's take my four considered fashion factors into account once again: organic, natural fibers, local, and social. At this level I am committed to filling three bases, and for any given base I will have two "unused" considered fashion factors waiting on the bench.

Let's look at a specific example: It's Valentine's Day, and I want to buy my guy a new pair of boxers. Because I am operating at the eco-warrior level I want to fill home, first, and second base. Thus, they have to have style, be made of natural fibers (first base), and also be made locally in the United States (second base). Sounds easy enough! And it is, because a friend of mine set out to satisfy those very criteria with a new men's basics line called Flint & Tinder. Done and done. My man gets a pair of sexy skivvies, and I get to be an eco-warrior.

Remember that social and organic are waiting on the bench, ready to go into play whenever I put them in. Thus, if it turned out that Flint & Tinder didn't manufacture their super-sexy male boxers here in the good ol' US of A, but if they were made of cotton and linked to a cause, they would still be a go. I would simply have switched out local for social on second base.

It is safe to say that you can confidently shop the mainstream fashion world operating at both the eco-citizen and eco-warrior level. More and more brands are redefining their brand missions to include social and environmental initiatives as part of the industry's evolution and, thus, are opening up options for shopping with style and sustainability built in.

Level Three (Third Base): Eco-Guru

Home: Style
1st Base:
2nd Base:
3rd Base:

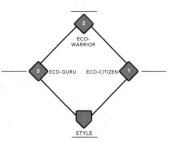

The eco-guru level requires a little more commitment than the other two levels. At this stage you're dedicated to securing four factors (and bases) for any given purchase and will create the Diamond Diagram at its upmost level. In my case the item must be stylish, made from natural fibers, made locally, and linked to a social cause or be organic to fill all four bases. When you get into this territory, the brands that can meet more than just a couple of considered fashion factors all at once are the brands that fall under the eco-fashion header. At the core of their existence is a mission to produce stylish pieces that also hit high environmental and social standards.

Many eco-fashion brands encompass numerous considered fashion factors by default, meaning they wouldn't do a production run and offer the collection without them being part of the supply chain. In essence, they do the heavy lifting by demanding these standards of themselves and the collections they offer to the public, and we reap the stylish fruits of their labor. For example, one of my favorite designers, David Peck, produces a super-stylish line called David Peck CROP in which the collection is inspired by a charitable cause that will be the recipient of a percentage of sales from that collection, is made from natural fibers (silk and organic cotton), and is made locally in Texas. One, two, three, four—score!

Peck also uses water-based dyes, so he hits yet another factor by de facto! With eco-brands this happens a lot. Their commitment to ethics, environmental, and social standards often automatically put them (and you) at the eco-guru purchasing level. For the sake of simplicity, I structured the Diamond Diagram in a diamond shape where the counter-clockwise filling of each base bumps your eco-level up until you fill all four and reach the "guru level." However, you can certainly add more factors for any given purchase and double-load the bases. This arrangement does occur fairly often with eco-brands.

Operating at the eco-guru level is very rewarding. You know that every purchase you make at this level supports a number of values you hold, and it feels amazing to literally wear that sentiment on your sleeve. Yet if you start at this level and don't find what you are looking for when seeking a certain garment or cut, start slow and go to the eco-warrior or eco-citizen level to get what you want. Through a flexible framework you can navigate these new and influential ways of supporting a fashionably considered lifestyle—yours. Now that you have the Integrity Index and Diamond Diagram in your arsenal, you're equipped to shop the world over in a conscious and style-savvy way. Part Two couples these tools with classic wardrobe and styling techniques to help you create a truly sustainable closet. Gentlemen, skip ahead to Chapter 8. Ladies, forge on to the next chapter!

PART
2

CHAPTER 4

FASHION FOUNDATION: A CLOSET FULL OF CLOTHES, BUT NOTHING TO WEAR

"I like my money right where I can see it . . . hanging in my closet."

—CARRIE BRADSHAW

You know that unsettling moment when you stand before your closet, doors wide open to reveal the inner contents, and you only have ten minutes to get dressed, which really feels impossible because, alas, you have absolutely nothing to wear? Yep, we've all been there. That situation has a couple of things going on. First, your closet may not be optimally organized to show you what you actually have and allow for ease when creating outfits. We are going to fix that with a closet-organizing exercise in this chapter. Second, there may be too much going on in that small (or rather spacious if you are lucky) closet space, and it might be time to look at rotating some of your clothes out each season, storing them properly and giving your closet some breathing room to show you just what your weather-appropriate options are.

Now, for most people those two quick fixes transform their wardrobes and their ability to get dressed each day and love what they are wearing. But you, my friend, are ready to level up. Have you heard that term? It is kind of a pop culture figure of speech that means if you are playing at one level where everything is working but not necessarily challenging yourself, it is time to level up. And with that leveling up comes increased experiences, resources, opportunities, and personal status. Leveling up here means that you recognize that the phrase "you are what you wear" has the outer meaning that refers to how you look and how you put your outfits together as well as the inner meaning that signifies that you care about where your clothes come from, who made them, with what materials, in what setting, under what conditions, and to the benefit of whom. To simplify, we can call this leveling up a vested interest in both the front story (visual and aesthetically pleasing) and backstory (who, what, where, why, and how).

Operating at this higher level does (initially) take a tad more energy and time, but I promise you it is well worth it and helps to propel you forward into a genuine space that honors who you are and how you present that self to the world. Wearing no evil is one part ethics (everything we went over in Chapters 2 and 3) and one part style. When you have a clear and strong sense of your style you make fewer fashion mistakes with your purchases, and that leads to a long-lasting, sustainable wardrobe.

To get started you will need to take a look at your closet through unbiased eyes. Some of us may need to recruit a friend to standby and give feedback as we do this. You can even pull that person up on Skype or FaceTime to show them pieces of your wardrobe that are questionable in order to get the "yay" or "nay." Also, check in with yourself about the factors you selected from the Integrity Index as the most important to you. If you can keep those five factors in the back of your mind as we move through these first two exercises, it will make the third exercise that much easier.

COLOR ME MINE

Before we jump into the closet-cleansing exercise, there are a couple of additional factors to consider: color and fit. We live in a colorful world bursting with vibrancy all around us, yet many of us are stuck in the neutral (or, more specifically, black) rut. Although neutrals and black are safe building blocks, we also need an infusion of color to better communicate who we are, highlight our best features, and lighten our mood. The Institute for Color Research reported that you are judged within the first ninety seconds of an initial viewing, and astonishingly 62 to 90 percent of that is based on color. Many people shy away from color because they don't know which ones to wear or steer clear of. There are colors that work better with certain skin tones than do others, and vice versa.

When you get it right your eyes light up, your skin flushes with a healthy glow, and your hair shines. You can get really in depth with what color way you are and what your best palette is; however, I am just going to graze the tip of the iceberg here and give you some simple guidelines to help you get started. If you decide you'd like to dive deeper, I would absolutely recommend you pick up a copy of *Life in Color* by Jesse Garza and Joe Lupo.

The first thing to determine is whether you have naturally warm or cool coloring. Answer the questions below as honestly as possible to find out.

Look at your inner wrist's veins. Which color do they resemble?
A. greenish   B. blueish

Find a mirror with natural lighting. Is your skin . . .
A. warm with a golden undertone   B. pale with blue undertones

When you get some sun do you . . .
A. tan (even if you freckle)   B. burn

Look at your eyes. Are they . . .
A. flecked with gold   B. clear or grayish blue, brown or green

Is your hair . . .
A. naturally highlighted   B. ashen based (ash blonde,
   with gold and red tones   or ash brown) or silver

If you answered mostly down the A column you are warm, and if you answered with more B's you are cool. So what does it all mean?

Warm

If you are warm you will want to embrace earth tones, which include: ivory (off-whites), khakis and browns, marigold yellow, burnt orange, orange-undertone reds and berry purples, moss and emerald green, cobalt blue, teal, and black.

Cool

Cool color ways look best in pastels and a few key jewel tones. Go for all variations of gray, mint green, pearly pink, powder blue, light lilac, periwinkle, bright turquoise, deep royal purple, coffee bean brown, true blue–based red, magenta, navy, and black.

While performing the exercises to cleanse your closet (we are almost there!), keep color in the back of your mind. You now know which colors best suit you, and it may be time to get rid of those that don't.

FIT

Proper fit is often overlooked, but it is one of the most essential pieces of the style puzzle to looking (and feeling) great. If you are like me, you probably have a number of items that aren't exactly your size, but they were on sale, so you bought them anyway. The only time this is truly acceptable is when you buy a size too large (shoes not included) and have it taken in and tailored to fit your body perfectly. In fact, as a general rule, you should buy pieces that fit your largest area (shoulders, hips, or belly) comfortably and accurately, and then tailor everything else to fit your skinnier limbs or narrow waist. You really cannot go the other way around. A dress that is too tight around the midsection is never going to help flatter your figure, no matter how short you make the skirt. Here are some general guidelines to follow for various body types in women:

Big on Top

Balance out your proportions with a bit more volume on the bottom half. Opt for wide or straight-leg trousers and A-line skirts that fall below the knee. Get an amazing bra to help manage your assets. V-necks (not too plunging, now) and the three-button blazer (which helps to keep the chest pulled in and creates a slim silhouette) are key.

Bigger in the Middle

Structured tops and bottoms with some added volume are your friend. Look for tops that incorporate an empire waist seam and then flow outward. That way you draw the eye toward your décolletage and hide the tummy under the extra material (though you needn't get carried away with super-billowy styles). Also, fitted jackets that close slightly above the natural waist are priceless. The popular peplum shape is also a great option, as it creates structure up top and flares out just above the stomach.

Bigger on the Bottom

Your goal is to bring the eye up, so look for tops that have interesting necklines or embellishments and come in vibrant hues. A pair of midrise straight-leg jeans or trousers are your key ingredient. Top things off with jackets that are made in heavier fabrics (like leather or tweed) to balance your overall look. When you wear skirts or dresses, don't try to hide your curves but instead embrace them with a form-fitting cut that falls just below the knee.

Flat All Over

We also call this the boy body shape because you don't have much in the way of boobs or a butt. However, this streamline frame is ripe for shaping. Go for clothing that hugs your body—we may even call it clingy. Create curves with peplums and jackets that flair out. Clothing with visible seaming and panels is another great way to bring visibility to your shape. Alternatively, this is the one body shape that looks good in slightly looser-fitting clothes like an off-the-shoulder T-shirt or sweater, or a flowy kaftan.

Curvy

Accentuating your waist is key. Look for shirts, jackets, and wrap dresses that all bring the focus to the midsection. Jackets and blazers should hit just at the hip or slightly lower. Opt for trousers that cinch closer to the natural waist (instead of low risers, which sit at the hips) with a straight leg in alignment with your hips' widest area.

So when you are cleansing your closet, take stock. What are the pieces that need to be tailored? Make a pile and actually take them to the tailor. Today. What are the pieces that no longer fit? Pass them on down the line. Our main objective is to clear out the clutter and make room only for pieces that sing your praises.

EXERCISE 1: CLOSET CLEANSE

Choose a day when you have a good amount of free time (at least two or three uninterrupted hours) to dive into this exercise. It is so wonderfully cathartic, and many Feng Shui masters will tell you that creating organized spaces helps to open up the flow of energy and allow for new things to come into your life. William Spear, the author of *Feng Shui Made Easy*, once said to me, "if your drawers, closets, and shelves are stuffed and overflowing in a disheveled mess, how can you expect the Universe to deliver anything more? There is no space for more!" The goal of this game is to evaluate, store, and purge.

Evaluate

This is the phase when you look at every single piece of clothing, jewelry, footwear, intimate apparel, and so forth in your closet. Think of this exercise as a closet detox, and after you've finished, your closet will be a good five to ten pounds lighter, with a clean, healthy glow. You can start section by section. Maybe take a look at all the pieces hanging in your closet first, and then move on to your drawers, and then your shoes. For every piece you pull out to evaluate, you will give it a yes, no, or maybe rating. You can start these corresponding piles on your bed or floor while you move through this sorting stage.

Yes. A yes item is something that you don't hesitate to keep. It is most likely a piece that you wear often or has some sentimental value. It feels great to recognize the pieces you know and love in your wardrobe, but take care to be honest with yourself about how often you actually wear them. If you haven't worn something for a couple of years, it is more likely destined for the maybe pile and more evaluation. Once you've established what your firm yeses are, you'll want to sort them according to season and then put them back into your closet and drawers in an easy-to-use, organized way. I will show you how to organize your closet for optimal use in the next section.

No. Saying no can be hard at first, and this is why I recommend you have a friend there with you who can give trusted and honest feedback. If you hesitate or are hard-pressed to remember the last time you wore the piece, it might be a no. If the piece still has the hangtag, has never been worn, and has been sitting in your closet for over a year, it is not for you. Let it go. If you pull out pieces that are ripped (unintentionally) and have wear and tear beyond repair, they too are nos.

If you find pieces in your closet that have been handed down or gifted to you that you did not select for yourself, and you can honestly say that you don't wear because they don't really reflect your style, they need to go into the no pile. Also, if you find pieces that are two sizes or more too big or too small, they need to go, and it is time to get new clothes that fit you and the body you have right now (not the body you will have once you lose ten pounds). Nos should be cleared out of your space entirely and can be donated to Goodwill and local thrift stores or placed in a clothing collection bin. If you do feel that some of the pieces in your no pile warrant a price (like quality designer goods), you can sell them through consignment shops, online, or enter them in clothing swaps.

WHAT TO DO WITH YOUR "NO" PILE

Donate. Perhaps the easiest way to discard old clothing you no longer want is to take it to a Goodwill store (check out goodwill.org for locations) or a Salvation Army shop (satruck.org) and donate it. Simply check their drop-off days and times and then make a trip. In many urban settings independent companies, like Wearable Collections (in the New York area), have set up collection bins within big doorman buildings, so you may not even have to leave home to donate. Across the United States USAgain (usagain.com) offers collection resources and even allows you to host a collection bin for your neighborhood. Lastly, use thethriftshopper.com to search a nationwide directory of thrift stores to find one near you to donate to.

Sell. If the pieces you are prepared to part with are designer or have some vintage value, try selling them before you donate them—you could make some extra cash in the process! There are numerous consignment shops in every community, so do a simple Google search or take a peek in the yellow pages. Additionally, there are quite a few successful online platforms you can list and sell on. I'll provide a whole list of those options in the following section.

Recycle. Sometimes the pieces you are throwing out are no longer suitable for you or anyone else to wear, but that doesn't mean that they should go to the landfill. More and more textile recycling companies and resources are popping up to offer a more responsible way to discard "end of life" clothing and textiles (e.g., towels, sheets, curtains). Here's what the EPA had to say about recycled textiles: "Textile recovery facilities separate overly worn or stained clothing into a variety of categories. Some recovered textiles become wiping and polishing cloths. Cotton can be made into rags or form a component for new high-quality paper. Knitted or woven woolens and similar materials are 'pulled' into a fibrous state for reuse by the textile industry in low-grade applications, such as car insulation or seat stuffing. Other types of fabric can be reprocessed into fibers for upholstery, insulation, and even building materials." Most textile collectors who are looking for wearable second-hand clothing will also have a relationship with a textile recycler who takes on their donations that are not wearable. Just ask. Another easy way to participate in textile recycling is to bring your discarded clothes to your local H&M. H&M has initiated a textile take-back program, called iCollect, where the public can bring used clothing (made from brands other than H&M too), and they will collect it and properly recycle it while giving you a discount voucher to use on your next H&M purchase.

....

Maybe. **Yes and no can be a little black and white, so sometimes you need a gray area. That is what the maybe pile is for. The maybe pile is a safe space for a second evaluation. So if you have a piece that was expensive or a gift and you don't really wear it but you're not sure you are ready to cut it loose, the maybe pile is a good holding place. Pretty much anything that is not a for-sure yes but you are unsure about straight-up getting rid of should go into this pile. I even tell my clients to make a maybe pile that they store and will reevaluate in three to six months' time. If it is still a maybe and you don't pull it out of the pile to wear it after not seeing it for a few months, you can confidently move it to the no pile.**

....

HOW TO HOST A CLOTHING SWAP

1. Choose a date (three to four weeks in advance and preferably during the weekend) and invite friends (ten to fifteen people). Aim for early spring or fall (when people are most likely to be looking for new clothes and cleaning out their closets).

2. Explain the rules (e.g., guests should bring up to ten items of clean clothes/accessories), and each item is valid for an exchange (leftover garments can be donated to a local charity/collection).

3. A week before the date, get organized! Find mirrors, clothing racks/tables/bins, and decide where your changing room will be (the bathroom? a bedroom?).

4. Decide which items you are going to swap. You can also separate items based on approximate value (low, medium, high), which would then correspond to a specific ticket color—your guests can do this upon arrival. Like-colored ticket items can be swapped out interchangeably, whereas lesser-value items (and ticket colors) can be used to add up to higher values for more "expensive" swaps. Make signs for the swaps so guests know where to place their items on arrival.

5. Decide on some light snacks, drinks, and music to enjoy during the party.

6. On the day, decorate! Replace wall hangings with special swap items, and decide how to separate the clothing (by value or category). Try to make it look like a pop-up shop.

Check out these websites for more information and opportunities to participate in swapping: swapstyle.com, events.swap.com, rehashclothes.com, dignswap.com, meetup.com.

....

EXERCISE 2: STORE OR SELL

Have you heard of rotating your wardrobe? I have been rotating my closet seasonally for the past few years, and it is an experience I always look forward to. Essentially, every time you clear out cold-weather clothing and bring in the warm-weather pieces you had stored, it is like getting a fresh new wardrobe! I also find that rotating clothing by season allows more space in your closet to display the currently wearable options without feeling pressure to prune the excess. For example, I love jackets. In the winter I have a number of jackets and coats that range in warmth so that I can dress appropriately for the outside temperatures. Yet those coats take up a lot of space, and if I were to keep them in my closet during the warmer months, I may feel the need to shrink my springtime blazer and leather jacket collection to keep my closet from getting too crowded. Think of rotating your wardrobe like eating what's in season. When it is hot out you'll grab some watermelon and a pair of wedge sandals, and when it is cold and dry you are likely to sip a warm soup and cozy up to an oversized scarf. Bottom line: seasons need not compete with each other if you organize and rotate properly.

PROPER STORING PRACTICES

The key to storing your clothing and accessories properly is to pack everything away nicely so that when you unpack they are ready to go. This goes without saying, but I am going to say it anyway: start with clean clothes, and if you need to do any touching up on your shoes or accessories, do that before you start packing. Find a couple of large, see-through Tupperware containers that will fit under the bed or stack neatly in a hall closet. These will become your "in-house" storage units, and you can label them by season.

Blazers and Jackets. I learned this trick from a guy friend who grew up going to a boarding school where they taught him the "correct way" to fold his blazer to keep it wrinkle-free. First, you turn your jacket inside out. Second, push one shoulder into the other shoulder (so that the jacket is now folded vertically in half and one shoulder is tucked inside of the other one). Finally, fold the jacket horizontally in half, and voilà! This is also a great trick to use when traveling and storing your jacket in the overhead compartment.

Blouses and Button-Downs. If you are packing away blouses or collared shirts that have already been ironed or are straight from the dry cleaners, you will want to use a piece of tissue paper to help keep wrinkles and creases to a minimum. Start with your shirt buttoned, and place it front down on the bed or table. Lay a piece of tissue paper vertically down the middle of the shirt. Fold the sleeves on top of the tissue, and then fold the whole shirt in half, turning it over to show the collar. Stack your shirts and blouses gently, giving them enough room to breathe. I also like to fold my dresses this way, with a piece of tissue; it helps keep them crisp and organized in storage.

Shoes, Handbags, Belts, and Jewelry. Here, too, you want to start with clean stock. So wipe down shoes, clean jewelry, and take pieces to be repaired if need be before you pack them up. Hopefully, you have saved any shoe or purse bags that came with your purchases so that you can use them now for storage. If not, or if you don't have enough, you can even use plastic shopping bags to store each item. It is important that each piece is wrapped up in a bag so that it stays clean and doesn't potentially "bleed" onto another piece.

Storing clothing not only works well for rotating your wardrobe but also for storing "maybes" that you will come back to later. In addition, I like to store DIY potentials (mostly from the maybe or no piles) for a day when I am feeling creative and crafty and want to reinvent one of my existing pieces of clothing. Finally, I use storage for any pieces that I've deemed too nice or expensive to give away or donate that I've listed online to try to sell and make some of my money back. There are a number of sites you can use to list items to sell and turn your closet into cash. These are my favorites:

Material Wrld: a curated community of influencers selling designer classics and on-trend updaters.

TreadFlip: a wider market place with unlimited access and listings that range from cheap thrills to designer investments.

Copious: started by a guy formerly at Facebook, this secondhand selling site plugs in all the social apps and has been one of the more successful selling platforms that I've used.

The Cools: a unique offering and community that celebrates independent designers and more original listings.

The Real Real: one of the best places to shop and sell authentic secondhand designer goods, including clothing, handbags, shoes, and jewelry.

Vaunte.com: an exclusive luxury online closet-sharing site that allows you to list and buy luxury goods . . . if you can score an invite to join!

EXERCISE 3: APPLY THE INTEGRITY INDEX

Now that you've fine-tuned your closet a bit, we can take a look at how your wardrobe measures up on the Integrity Index and, more specifically, against the five considered factors you've deemed most important. To help you through this stage, I'll use my own wardrobe as an example.

Remember, my top five considered fashion factors from the Integrity Index are as follows: natural fibers, local, linked to a social cause, organic, and style (the nonnegotiable!). I also highlight secondhand as an Integrity Index factor here, because so much of my parlay into eco-fashion started in that realm. Here is what a snippet of my closet run-through looks like:

ITEM	BRAND	MAKE	INTEGRITY
ethnic print top	French Connection	polyester, made in China	style
black stretch jeans (secondhand)	bebe	cotton, rayon, spandex, made in USA	style, second life, local
black blazer	J.Crew	wool, spandex, polyester, made in China	style
bikini swimsuit	Olga Olsson	spandex, ethically made in Brazil	style, socially linked
striped tank top	Express	cotton, modal, made in China	style, natural fibers
little black dress	Zara	cotton, spandex, made in Turkey	style
silk top	Sandro	100 percent silk, made in Tunisia	style, natural fibers
button down	Ralph Lauren	100 percent cotton, made in China	style, natural fibers
print summer dress	David Peck	organic cotton, made in USA, linked to charity	style, organic, natural fibers, local, social
loafers (secondhand)	Prada	leather, rubber, made in Italy	style, second life

Let's say that this snippet is an accurate representation of my entire wardrobe. We can see that three out of every ten items don't make the Integrity Index cut because they only have the style factor to boast about without coupling with any other considered fashion factor. To operate on even the first level, or eco-citizen level, in merging fashion with ethics, I would need to satisfy at least two considered fashion factors from the Integrity Index. As you can see, some of my pieces certainly do satisfy that quota. And some of them go above and beyond, hitting five factors at once! Although one-third of my wardrobe doesn't accurately represent me and my values with style, two-thirds of my closet does.

What should I do with the one-third that isn't ethically aligned with me? Keep it. Even though some (or even a lot, at first) of your pieces don't line up with you and your values, I am not suggesting you go out and buy a whole new wardrobe or even that you give up some of the core pieces in your wardrobe because they don't hit enough of the Integrity Index factors. To the contrary, I suggest you cherish those pieces you already have and love and make a pact with yourself that any new purchases will include two or more Integrity Index factors. That way you continue to build a strong foundation for your wardrobe on pieces that work for your body type and lifestyle while incorporating new pieces to fill any gaps or help update your wardrobe with your new heightened awareness toward shopping. Before long you will notice that every time you get dressed you are automatically incorporating at least one "eco-chic" piece by default because your wardrobe is naturally growing in an authentic wear-no-evil way.

As you now know, there are many more factors, and mine may not match up with yours, but the point is to show you how to start incorporating eco-awareness into your shopping habits and wardrobe without feeling overwhelmed. So, to keep things simple, start with the top five factors you've selected and use them as your guides. Exercise 3 is not meant to discourage you but rather to give you a sense of where you stand and to inspire you to commit to your selected considered fashion factors each and every time you shop so that your wardrobe authentically depicts both your style and ethics. Now it is your turn. Randomly choose ten pieces in your closet to apply the Integrity Index to (like I did in the example above) to see where you stand.

ITEM	BRAND	MAKE	INTEGRITY

CLOSET REHAB

Now that you have sorted, stored, and taken stock, it is time to put your closet back together. If rotating your clothes seasonally seems like too much work or you don't have enough clothes to warrant the quarterly move, you may want to start with changing things out every spring and fall. Either way, you will need to invest the time to get organized.

A clean and well-organized closet helps you put your best sartorial foot forward with confidence and ease. There are many ways to organize a closet, and I've combined a couple of my favorite methods to yield the best results.

1. Start with a clean, empty space. Take everything out of your closet and place it on the bed. Then go in with the vacuum and a dust rag to wipe down all shelves and clean the floors and corners.

2. Add shelves, dividers, shoe cubbies, lined basket drawers, and so on. You are the master of your own closet, so regardless of the size, you can make the most of the space you have and create places to hang items, fold them, and group them. You may also want to add some signature touches by putting down shelf paper and adding scented cedar blocks or an unlit candle.

3. Use Slimline Hangers (they'll give you twice as much space as standard wooden ones), and start hanging the pieces you wear most. You may find you live in dresses. If that is the case, they should be hanging front and center in the middle of your closet. From there, hang your tops to one side of your dresses and trousers to the other. Alternatively, blouses and button-downs may be your thing. Hang them in the center, bookending them with trousers and dresses.

4. Group your garments. Dresses go together, as do jeans, as do jackets . . . you get the picture. Within each grouping you'll want to organize by color. I tend to start with white and beige, then move toward yellow, orange, green, and pink. Next, red, blue, gray, brown, and black. It is also helpful to organize by style. Let's take the dress example again. Start with strapless and move through to long sleeve. Also, don't worry about length; color and style are more important in terms of organization.

5. Sweaters. Hanging is the best way to put your pieces on display, but sweaters are the exception. When you hang a sweater it will likely take on the shape of the hanger and loose its own shape. Choose a couple of shelves to house folded sweaters. Again, color coordinate, and you may find you have one pile with more lightweight sweaters (color coded from light to dark) and a separate pile with heavier styles.

6. Trousers, skirts, and shorts. These should always be hung, and use proper skirt hangers so that you can easily see the shape and cut when selecting what to wear.

7. Jeans. I like to fold my jeans. I just feel like they get lost in the trouser section when they should have their own designated area. A stacked pile of light to dark works well. Some people find that folding them so that the back pocket is visible at the fold is also helpful; this is key when you have multiple pairs in the same-ish wash and need to differentiate.

8. T-shirts. If you have the shelf space, divide them into color-coded piles of "nice" and "knock around." If you don't have shelf space, you can roll them and keep them in a drawer. By rolling and lining them up, they stay more visible than stacking them in a drawer, where you only see the one that is on top.

9. Bags and scarves. A top shelf is prime real estate for your bag collection. Take your bags out of their dust bags (reserve them for when you store your bags or travel) and line them up according to size/style and color. Nicely folded scarves belong on a shelf that is waist- to eye-level high; that way you can see all the colors and quickly grab one to complete your look.

10. Jewelry. Dedicate either dresser space (on top) or a midlevel closet shelf to jewelry. Create or buy lined shelves with lots of little compartments to set your jewelry out. If it is packed away, you won't see it, so you won't wear it. Get a small corkboard and hang necklaces over pushpins from it. Some women also like to use small dishes around the house (next to the bed, in the bathroom, or on the entryway console table) so that they can easily grab a pair of earrings or some bangles as a last-minute touch before heading out.

11. Hats. These are top-shelf renters too. Try to keep them in hatboxes, and affix a Polaroid or printed-off picture to the outside so you know what is in there.

12. Shoes. Cubby shelves are my favorite for shoes. It creates a special space for them, which I think they warrant. Organize them by color and style (wedges with wedges, heels with heels, boots with boots). Another trick is to position one shoe with the toe forward and the other with the heel forward, so that for each pair you know what the shoe looks like (front and back) at a glance.

13. Active wear. My active wear lives in drawers—the deeper the better. I will use one drawer for all my yoga, running, and tennis attire (including sports bras and visors), and another drawer for the heavier layers (like hooded sweatshirts).

By the end of this chapter you should feel that you have a good grasp on the pieces that make up your wardrobe. You may also start to see what pieces you are lacking. The next few chapters are designed to help guide your purchases, with both style and ethics in mind, and help you fill in the gaps to create a well-rounded wardrobe with plenty of options.

CHAPTER 5

STYLE SORTED, LADIES: SHOES, BOTTOMS, TOPS, DRESSES, AND ACCESSORIES

"Some have theorized that the innate style of a French girl is so superior to that of her American counterparts because she lives by a closet code that allows only five items a season: good pants, a good shirt, a good dress, a good jacket, and good shoes."

—LEANDRA MEDINE

They say that style cannot be taught, but I disagree. In a way we are always questing to find what suits us: what makes us stand tall, with confidence and poise; which colors compliment our skin, hair, and eyes; what shapes flatter our natural stature; and what handbag speaks loud and clear as an extension of ourselves. And all of these pieces that make up our collective style are learned. The point I want to emphasize is that they are all different for each of us. There is no formula. Sure, there are basics that every woman should own (that just makes getting dressed easier), but how you put your look together, what colors you choose, and any signature attributes you affix are your own. They help to define you and instill that boom-boom-pow confidence that is the most attractive of all.

Yet fashion is a trillion-dollar industry, and with so many options to choose from, it is easy to feel overwhelmed. Don't. These next few chapters are dedicated to guiding you through every area of your wardrobe with style advice, go-green guides, and some of my personal recommendations on brands that deliver solid style and ethics simultaneously.

I know I sound like your third-grade teacher, but beauty really does come from within. When you love yourself and celebrate who you are, recognizing your so-called flaws as the keys to your individuality, you radiate an infectious sense of self-worth that is the cornerstone to having great style. Everyone has hang-ups about their body. You are always your harshest critic. Yet when you stop fighting your way to be the media's status quo perfect woman (who closely resembles a Victoria's Secret model), you get real and start highlighting what makes you beautiful. We all have people in our lives who inspire us, and if you pinpoint it to one thing that makes them so attractive, it is their comfort and ease in their own skin.

Take ownership of your body. Keep yourself fit and healthy. You don't need to strive to look like anyone other than the self-loved and looked-after version of your best self. There is a powerful energy that flows through and around you when you take the time and dedicate willpower to care for yourself. I have my parents to thank for a lot things, and one of them is their combined svelte bone structure and high metabolisms. One gangly, skinny guy chose a Twiggy-looking girl to be his wife, and their offspring had no choice but to be small boned and very skinny. Growing up, my nickname was Toothpick. Fifteen years later not a lot has changed. I honestly think my body is the same as it was in high school, and this is both a blessing and a curse. It is a blessing because I don't really have to regulate what I eat or even exercise to maintain a body shape that is familiar and desirable to me. It is a curse because that often leaves me skinny but also unfit and unhealthy.

It took me a couple of years of living the New Yorker workaholic, no-time-for-anything-else lifestyle to realize how unhappy I was with myself and how I had lost the self-confidence I had all through school (high school, college, and grad school), when I proactively made exercise a part of my routine and identity. Luckily, I am back on track, and my aging heart, bones, and muscles thank me. I tell this story simply to illustrate that clothes are half the battle. When you actively seek to keep up the body you've been given (what Buddhists call the temple) with a healthy, balanced diet and exercise, your confidence and luminosity shine from within, and clothes fit better.

Many movies, TV shows, and magazine articles romanticize the art of getting dressed, and often an interviewing journalist is disappointed when I reveal that the weather is the dictating factor for what I choose to wear each day. Call me a pragmatist, but I like to be stylish *and* comfortable. So start with the weather. When you know what the weather will be like, you can plan which shoes are best suited for that and then go from there. There is nothing worse than being stuck in the rain with inadequate shoes or sweating it out on a hot day with shoes that don't breathe. Every stylist knows that the key to making an outfit work is a great pair of shoes. They have the ability to transform a ho-hum look into something elegant and fashion forward with every step.

Style Secret: Putting a look together works best from the bottom up.

PRICE CHECK

Throughout this chapter use this key to gauge the price point of any item easily.

....

$ - - - - - - - - - $0–$50

$$ - - - - - - - - $50–$150

$$$ - - - - - - - $150–$350

$$$$ - - - - - - $350+

SHOES

During my time in London I read an article by a fashion writer who said that if you do nothing else, invest in your shoes. When you buy quality (and this often means designer) shoes, they fit better, last longer, and are always more comfortable (heels included!). That made a lasting impression, and personal experience has backed up that simple statement. After a break up I took my sad self to Selfridges and bought a black pair of Marc Jacobs Mary Jane pumps. A classic case of retail therapy, I wore those shoes almost every day for a year while my heart healed and my confidence grew. I was so surprised at how I could wear them all day (and sometimes all night). I still own those shoes and wear them often. They are one of the best purchases I've ever made, and their designer quality and comfort have made them a sustainable investment.

A lot of women are shoe obsessed, and if shoes are your thing, by all means indulge in your passion. For the rest of us, there are just a few shoe staples to include in your wardrobe to ensure you have options that suit every occasion—and forecast.

Green Guide: Vegan or Leather? There are various eco-credentials to look for when shopping for shoes. An easy way to start is to opt for vegan shoes. Either for humanitarian or environmental reasons, many people are drawn to shopping vegan. Canvas, cork, rubber, and faux leather are all great options when shopping vegan. If vegan is one of your leading Integrity Index factors, you are clear on your shopping parameters, and I am pleased to say that the options are growing. Yet I would caution that vegan options are not always environmentally better than their leather counterparts, as they sometimes use man-made materials that can wind up being toxic.

I recently received a pair of vegan shoes from JustFab.com, and when I took them out of the box my entire room filled with a toxic synthetic smell. Then, as I looked at the return slip, there was a disclaimer at the bottom of the sheet that read, "Warning: this product contains chemicals known to the state of California to cause cancer, or birth defects or other reproductive harm." Yikes! The other hesitation I have toward vegan shoes is their longevity. They tend to run a shorter lifespan than do leather shoes, which age nicely and break in over time. This is a conversation a lot of my eco-conscious colleagues and I have been having, and there seems to be no clear-cut answer. Of course, it is a personal choice, and ultimately *you* decide what you'd like to support with your purchasing. Perhaps it will be a little of both until better vegan options evolve.

For me, my preference is to buy quality shoes made from (mostly) natural materials produced in safe and fair working conditions that support a local community of artisans. There are new brands popping up all the time with these criteria down pat. Osborn Design is one such brand. As they say, "we make beautiful things in beautiful ways." Each collection is designed in Green Point, Brooklyn, and then materials and labor are sourced from artisans in South America, creating a tight infrastructure for quality production and an uncompromising commitment to traditional craft. To green your shoe shopping even more, you can also look for smaller brands that use vegetable-tanned leathers and upcycled materials and use sustainably sourced natural resources for their production in addition to fair-trade standards.

What About Mainstream Designer Shoes?

As I've already shared in my retail therapy Marc Jacobs story, designer shoes tend to hold their value as a sustainable investment over time. Given the option to purchase a cheap pair of faux-leather shoes or designer shoes (both are likely made in China, by the way), I would choose the designer shoes and even save up a little longer in order to make that investment purchase. What would be even better would be to purchase the designer shoes secondhand. That way you know you are getting quality that will stand the test of time, and you are giving a discarded pair a second lifecycle.

That said, if secondhand shoes kind of creep you out (I've never had a problem), the highest ground to take is to purchase quality shoes made by independent designers and artisans. To find those brands, you simply need to ask. When you look at a brand's website and read their "about" story, you can start to piece together how and where their shoes are made. Also, try to shop locally in smaller boutiques. These boutiques usually carry more bespoke and smaller designer lines as part of their curated offering.

Types of Shoes

Flats. Any woman can attest to the practicality of owning a great pair of flats. From day to day life to running through airports to catch a plane, flats certainly have their place. The key to choosing a pair of flats that compliment your style instead of dilute it is to focus on the details. A beautiful pair of flats in an interesting color, like burnt orange or metallic silver, add an understated punch to your overall look. Bows, tassels, bejeweled embellishments, and texture (like snakeskin or leopard print) all contribute to a more intentional and put-together feel. Try to incorporate three to four pairs of flats in your wardrobe so you can rotate them and adjust according to the weather and what look and feel you are going for (casual or smart). As you build your wardrobe you will likely want to invest in the various flat styles (ballet, boat shoe, slip-on sneaker, etc.). It will give you greater outfit options and ease when getting dressed. To start, though, I would suggest you purchase one pair of ballet flats, dressy sandals, flip flops, and sneakers.

Style Secret: Transform your flat footwear with foot lingerie. By adding a neon pop of color or a classy touch of lace, you subtly broadcast your savvy style sense.

Heels. Seductive and empowering, the heel can add instant sex appeal or authority, and usually both! The height that comes with a heel gives a confidence boost while lengthening your legs, straightening your posture, and letting you feel that much more dressed up and put together. I recommend a pair of strappy heels for summer and a closed-toed (perhaps even pointy) pair for colder months.

Style Secret: If you are getting dressed for an important event, meeting, or appearance, plan out what you want to wear the night before. It can be so stressful trying on options the morning of when the clock is ticking down to your seeming demise. And actually try things on. You need to know how it all comes together. Believe me, you will sleep more soundly knowing that your outfit is pitch perfect.

Boots. During the fall and winter, boots are absolutely essential and such a fun way to create new looks within your existing wardrobe. To start, you will need one pair of flats and one pair that give you a lift, either through a heel or wedge. The flat pair can act as your go-to boot for when the weather is poor and the streets slick, whereas a wedge or heeled version lets you dress up during cool weather and still be comfortable. As with the other shoes categories, you'll likely find that having one of each of the various boot styles (ankle, riding, motorcycle, etc.) gives greater flexibility when getting dressed, so don't be afraid to invest in various pairs over time.

SHOES

WHO TO SHOP	INTEGRITY RATING	DIAMOND LEVEL	PRICE
Timberland (Earthkeepers Collection)	upcycled/recycled materials	eco-citizen	$$$
Cri de Coeur	vegan	eco-citizen	$$$
Freda Salvador	local	eco-citizen	$$$
Terhi Pölkki	local, natural materials	eco-warrior	$$$$
Melissa Plastic Shoes	recycled/recyclable	eco-citizen	$$

JEANS AND TROUSERS

I don't know a woman today who doesn't own a pair of jeans. When you find the right fit they are simply magical. Over time jeans have become more widely viewed as an acceptable option for various occasions. I don't think we will see them on the red carpet any time soon, but never say never. These days you can comfortably wear them from day to night and be perfectly dressed for all your goings-on, save more formal affairs. The other great thing about jeans is that they span effortlessly across different age groups.

Trousers and jeans share a variety of cuts and styles, and typically you will want to include two to three of these differing versions in your closet to give yourself enough options. Remember to apply the rules of dressing for your body type (chapter 4) to get the best fit and overall shape, but it is safe to say that owning four styles of jeans/trousers will get you by with style and ease. These four staple styles include: skinny, straight leg, high-waisted wide leg, and cropped.

Green Guide: When shopping for jeans, the leading eco-credentials to look for are reduced water use (remember, the average pair of jeans takes seven hundred gallons of water to produce), nonchemical finishing treatments, made from organic cotton or made from recycled/upcycled materials, and made locally (in the country you live in).

Skinny Jeans and Trousers. The skinny cut is a modern-day must-have. The slim fit pairs perfectly with ballet flats, flat sandals, wedges, and boots. Wear them with a relaxed T-shirt, leather jacket, and a pair of boots or flats. The result is an effortlessly cool outfit. Skinny trousers made from cotton, wool, and silk are the dressed up cousin of the skinny jean and can help you create the same shape and outfit options with more of a refined feel. Colored jeans and trousers in the skinny style have become very popular and are a great way to liven up your look.

My advice is to get one pair of dark-wash skinny jeans, one pair of colored skinny jeans, and one pair of black skinny trousers. You can add a pair of skinny print pants if you are feeling more adventurous and know that you will actually incorporate them into how you dress. Over time you may naturally expand your wardrobe, but those are a great place to start.

Straight Leg or Bootcut. Have you ever observed a woman wearing a pair of jeans that not only make her butt look good but also give the optical illusion that her legs go on for miles? Either she is a supermodel or she is wearing a pair of straight-leg jeans with heels tucked discreetly underneath. The cut of a straight-leg or bootcut jean keeps a slim fit all the way down the leg and either continues with a straight cut or a slight flare (in the bootcut style) to allow you to pull the cuff of the pant leg over the back of your shoe, making this the key style of jean to pair nicely with heels (platforms and wedges included). If you need some inspiration, look to Victoria Beckham. She has built her whole identity around this style of jean.

For a dressier option this cut looks great in a wool or cotton blend in dark and jewel-toned colors. Here, I would suggest owning one pair of straight-leg jeans in a safe wash (nothing too wild or with distressed detailing) and one pair of black or dark-colored trousers in a color that works best with your coloring and wardrobe. This pant style is very versatile, and you'll be amazed how many options you'll have with just a couple of pairs.

Style Secret: The heels + straight-leg jean + dressy top + fitted jacket combo was popularized over a decade ago but doesn't have to look dated if you keep your accessories and hair current. It is an outfit combo that works on every body type and is becoming a classic look for the modern-day woman.

High-Waisted Wide Leg. Unless you are already exceptionally tall, the high-waisted wide-leg combo is the solution to creating balanced proportions that flatter almost every body type while also adding height. The higher the waist and the wider the leg, the more 1970s the feel, and that certainly works for some women's style identity and aesthetic. Think Nicole Richie here. A more toned-down version is perfect for the work place. Just like the straight-leg cut, you will want to style them with shoes that add height, a nice top, and a cropped jacket or blazer. Throw on a statement necklace, and your look is perfectly polished.

Style Secret: The key to wide-leg trousers is to keep them long enough that they essentially cover your entire shoe and slightly sweep the ground as you walk. Also, because there is so much volume on the bottom with this style, keep your top cinched in and tailored. Cropped and fitted jackets are the perfect compliment.

Cropped. In my mind, cropped equals classic. The shape is synonymous with style icons such as Audrey Hepburn and Grace Kelly. However, they must be worn correctly to convey the ease and elegance they truly embody. Today, you can look to Olivia Palermo for a modern take on how to sport this timeless cut. Getting it right is all about where the pant leg hits. Too high, and they can make you look shorter; too long, and it just looks like you have an ill-fitting pair of trousers that the tailor butchered. The most flattering place for the pant to fall is the sweet spot where you ankle meets your calf muscle. To create a tasteful look, pair a boxy sweater top with a three-quarter-length sleeve and a pair of pointed-toe sling-back heels, and finish with a pair of cat eye or oversized sunglasses. Perfection.

JEANS AND TROUSERS

WHO TO SHOP	INTEGRITY RATING	DIAMOND LEVEL	PRICE
Monkee Genes	organic, fair trade, local	eco-guru	$$
Levi's Water<Less line	lower water footprint	eco-citizen	$$
IOU Project	fair trade, transparent, upcycled details	eco-guru	$$
7 For All Mankind	local	eco-citizen	$$$
Agave Denim	local	eco-citizen	$$$

TOPS

For some reason I find that picking the right top to complete an outfit always presents more of a challenge than I want it to. Everything can be coming together nicely, then you add a top that doesn't quite mesh, and it all goes horribly wrong. You can easily side step this daily obstacle by building a wardrobe full of varied options to compliment your bottom half. Any fashion editor or stylish woman will confidently list off the tops they can't live without, and I've scoured their lists to help compile the ultimate index of tops to include in your wardrobe.

Green Guide: Shopping for tops will encompass such a wide range of styles, cuts, fabrics, and weights. It is important to look into your existing closet, weed out the pieces that you don't wear or that don't actually flatter your body type, and then keep an eye out whenever you go shopping to fill in the gaps for a more complete closet. Very often on a lunch break or when I am out running errands, I will pop into a secondhand store to see what "new" tops they've recently received. I'll keep a running tab of items I am looking for on my phone and check it before I go into the store to focus my shopping intentions.

A word about shopping secondhand: if you shop the stores that are located in a wealthier area, they are more likely to carry quality designer brands that are made from luxury fibers, which will look more expensive and hold up well over time. It is far better to make an investment in even these secondhand luxury items than to opt for five other poly-blend tops at a cheaper thrift store. The only time I do encourage my clients to shop these cheaper charity shops is when they want to try out a new trend and don't want to spend a lot of money doing so. This is a good option for deciding whether a cut or pattern works on you, and if it does, then the next one you buy should be of a higher quality (which usually comes with a higher price tag).

I would recommend starting with secondhand shopping for tops because you find so many great pieces (some have never been worn!) and can easily build up your wardrobe options without breaking the bank. Otherwise, the next best thing is to look for brands and designers who use natural or sustainable fibers, local production, and vegetable dyes. Most often you will find that easy-to-wear tops like T-shirts, tanks, and long-sleeve shirts are made with Tencel, organic cotton, silk, hemp, or linen. Alternatively, tees made from recycled plastic are readily available too. Of course, a well-rounded wardrobe includes some more dressed-up options like a classic white button-down, a cashmere cardigan, a sequin top, and a couple of blouses. You'll find recommendations for all of these below.

Building-Block Tops

Most women already have a number of items that fall into this category. The question is: Do you have the right ones? There is a careful balancing act associated with casual dressing and the pieces you use to create your overall look. Throwing on any old worn-in T-shirt from high school won't do (unless you are going to the gym). However, striking this ideal balance is easier than you think when you have key pieces to help you get there.

Building blocks are not the show stoppers. They are the nondescript yet perfectly cut and colored pieces that help pull it all together. Think neutrals here. Navy, white, heather or stone gray, and black are the colors you should be looking for in a great-fitting V-neck tee or long racerback tank. Additionally, every woman should own a Breton-striped boatneck long-sleeve or three-quarters-sleeve tee. These pieces alone will supply endless outfit combos that exude a casual, cool confidence.

T-shirts also present a distinct canvas for displaying your support for a beloved rock band (vintage concert tees never go out of fashion), social causes (the brand A Lot To Say gives you tons of options), or even your favorite cartoon character. I tend to steer left of slogan tees and opt for their clean-cut brethren, but it is always nice to have a couple of them in the closet when the occasion to wear one strikes.

TEES AND TANKS

WHO TO SHOP	INTEGRITY RATING	DIAMOND LEVEL	PRICE
Pickwick & Weller	local, natural fibers (some organic)	eco-warrior	$$
Everlane	local, natural fibers	eco-warrior	$
Organic by John Patrick	natural fibers, organic, fair trade	eco-guru	$$
Alternative Apparel	low impact dyes	eco-citizen	$
Stateside	natural fibers, local (some organic)	eco-warrior	$$

BRETON-STRIPE TEES AND LONG-SLEEVE TOPS

WHO TO SHOP	INTEGRITY RATING	DIAMOND LEVEL	PRICE
Ekyog	organic, fair trade	eco-warrior	$$
Amour Vert	local, organic	eco-warrior	$$
Study NY	local, organic, natural fibers	eco-guru	$$

Dressed-Up Tops

Sometimes that tee won't cut it, and you'll need something a little more refined for the occasion. Collared button-downs and silk blouses are my go-tos. They are perfect for the workplace and lend a bit of masculine simplicity. A classic white button-down, which is fitted and comes in slightly to hug your waist, is an absolute must. It can go dressy or casual with a tailored skirt and heels or a pair of skinny jeans and ballet flats, respectively. Silk blouses are excellent for bringing a pop of color or print to your ensemble. They look fabulous paired with a pencil skirt or slim-cut trousers.

The other dress-up staples include an embellished fitted tank, a sequin top (check your local vintage shop for racks and racks to choose from), and a lace top (which you should wear over a nude or black stretchy tank). Again, these tops are very versatile and can be worn effortlessly with skirts or jeans.

BLOUSES AND BUTTON DOWNS

WHO TO SHOP	INTEGRITY RATING	DIAMOND LEVEL	PRICE
Carrie Perry	local, natural fibers, organic, recycled	eco-guru	$$$
Svilu	natural fibers, organic, local	eco-guru	$$$
Maiyet	social, natural fibers	eco-warrior	$$$
Heidi Merrick	natural fibers, local	eco-warrior	$$$
The Podolls	local, natural fibers, organic, fair trade	eco-guru	$$$

FANCY TOPS

WHO TO SHOP	INTEGRITY RATING	DIAMOND LEVEL	PRICE
Minna	zero waste, organic, upcycled, local	eco-guru	$$$
Behnaz Sarafpour	organic fabrics, local	eco-warrior	$$$$
Obakki	local, social	eco-warrior	$$$

PRINT TOPS

WHO TO SHOP	INTEGRITY RATING	DIAMOND LEVEL	PRICE
Partimi	organic fibers, natural dyes, local	eco-guru	$$$$
Althea Harper	local, organic fabrics (check garment to garment)	eco-warrior	$$$
Steven Alan	local, natural fibers	eco-warrior	$$$
ASOS Africa	social	eco-citizen	$
Feral Childe	local, natural fibers, organic	eco-guru	$$

Style Secret: Making prints work for you is all about finding a beautiful print that is in your color way (see Chapter 4). The size of the print may vary from small to big, and if you get the coloring right, it will become a special addition to your wardrobe and help you stand out when desired (i.e., at a cocktail party or a work conference).

SWEATERS AND HOODIES

In the winter and on cool summer nights a soft and comfy layer is just the thing. There is something so luxurious about being swaddled in cashmere on a cold day, during a long flight, or while watching a movie at the theater. As you can tell, my preference in this category is to buy cashmere, and my reasons are twofold: number one, it is wonderfully soft and feels great against your skin, and number two, it is one of the warmest natural fibers out there. Cashmere wool blends are good too, and you will also often see a cashmere-silk-blend option.

I like to have at least one longer, loose-fitting V-neck sweater, a slouchy boyfriend cardigan (longer cut with buttons and two pockets in the front—looks great belted), a classic fitted cardigan, and a turtleneck sweater in my winter wardrobe. A boyfriend cardigan and long V-neck sweater look great with trousers or a short mini and loafers (when the weather warms). A classic cardi is perfect for throwing over a dress or a tee with jeans. The turtleneck sweater recently became a favorite of mine. It gives an instant Audrey Hepburn flair and looks so chic with a pair of cropped black trousers and flats.

Green Guide: Stay with the natural fibers (and don't muddy the waters with synthetics), and you are good to go. Take your eco-creds a little further by making sure the brands you purchase openly show their supply chain and support ethical production and treatment of animals. You get bonus points if they use vegetable dyes to achieve their colors.

SWEATERS, CARDIGANS, AND TURTLENECKS

WHO TO SHOP	INTEGRITY RATING	DIAMOND LEVEL	PRICE
Stewart + Brown	local, fair trade, veg dyed	eco-guru	$$$
Blake London	fair trade, local, natural fibers	eco-guru	$$$
DKNY Pure	natural fibers	eco-citizen	$$$
Chinti & Parker	organic	eco-citizen	$$$
M.Patmos	organic, fair trade, natural fibers, local	eco-guru	$$$

Hoodies and Sweatshirts

In Victoria Beckham's style book *That Extra Half an Inch*, she boldly christened the zip-up hoodie as the new leather jacket or blazer. I happen to agree, albeit, I would preface that the zip-up hoodie is the dressed-down version of these other staple layers. They look great over your morning yoga outfit while you pick up your Yerba Mate latte. They can also act as an edgy layer under a leather jacket worn with a tee, shorts, tights, and boots (we can thank Parisian models for that staple outfit). And I don't have to tell anyone that they are the perfect around-the-house layer.

Green Guide: Going green with hoodies can go one of two ways: you can stay with the natural or sustainable (i.e., biodegradable) fibers, like I suggested with sweaters, cardis, and turtlenecks, or you can find a number of options made from recycled PET. Champion was the first brand to make a hooded zip sweatshirt to keep NYC warehouse workers warm, and so it is exciting to note that this pioneer has an eco-offering made from recycled polyester in their eco range. The sweatshirt (sans hood) is also making a fashion comeback as a casual staple to pair with a leather (or pleather, if that is your preference) mini or a skinny pair of jeans. The brands below are my favorites in this category.

HOODIES AND SWEATSHIRTS

WHO TO SHOP	INTEGRITY RATING	DIAMOND LEVEL	PRICE
Champion, eco line	recycled PET	eco-citizen	$
Marine Layer	natural fibers, local	eco-warrior	$$
Patagonia	recycled PET, fair trade	eco-warrior	$$
Alternative Earth	low impact dyes, organic, upcycled, fair trade	eco-guru	$$$
Groceries	local, organic	eco-warrior	$

SKIRTS AND DAY DRESSES

Skirts are essential, at least in my wardrobe. The length of the skirt is pretty well proportioned to age—the older you get, the longer they become. Yet I would say that skirt length truly is a personal choice and, of course, should be based on where you are going (e.g., no short minis in church). If your legs are one of your more celebrated attributes, wearing a shorter variety can become a signature style statement.

Day dresses are little slices of heaven, aren't they? They are so easy to throw on and transform your entire look and feel. A casual one is perfect for running weekend errands or heading to the beach, and one that is a bit more structured is flawless for the office. The best part is how breathable and flexible they are.

Green Guide: The cut and style of a dress or skirt will dictate the fabrics used. Maxi or flowing dresses and skirts tend to run on the purer side of things. Designers don't need them to stretch around your body because the style is more loose fitting to begin with. When you are shopping for these styles, look for brands that are produced using 100 percent natural, organic, or sustainable fabrics (like Tencel and modal) as well as vegetable dyes. You can also find brands upholding all of those standards plus the "Made in the USA" badge. That is your best bet.

If you are looking for more of a form-fitting shift dress or tight pencil skirt, then you will have to allow for the use of some synthetics, as they provide the elastic and flexible shape to these styles. Again, if you look for brands that use organic materials, nontoxic dyes, and local production, you still come out on top. The designer has already made the tough call for you. Chances are they didn't want to use the spandex or nylon either, but by not including just a little (sometimes we are talking about 4 percent), the style of their garment would suffer, as would your appearance. So they chose to do their best and still create a piece that is fashionable as well as considered. Thank you, designers!

If you are really adamant about no synthetics, your other option is to buy the looser-fitting dresses and belt them. I have a number of beautiful and vibrantly colored silk dresses that on the hanger look like a wide sleepwear tunic, but when I add a belt and a pair of heels they are dynamite.

Additionally, one of my favorite resources for dresses is RentTheRunway.com. A couple of gals from Harvard Business School created an online store that offers designer dresses in different sizes that can be rented for a period of four or eight days at a time. You select what dress you want to wear and the dates you'd like to rent it (you can also select a backup dress for a little extra). Then they mail the dress to you (in two sizes, plus your backup dress if you've added one) to try on and wear to your event. When you are done, you simply place them in the provided return mailer and pop them into a mailbox. I have used them for countless weddings, fancy dress events, and even for hosting. I love knowing that I didn't have to buy a new dress only to wear it once, and instead I am sharing the same dress with hundreds (maybe thousands!) of other women. Now, *that* is sustainable!

Skirts

A well-rounded wardrobe only needs a few skirts. If you like to show off your legs, a mini is a must (sequin, leather or pleather, and denim are all excellent options). The tulip-shaped skirt has a high waist and pleats that create volume in the middle before slimming back in toward the knee. This cut is very flattering on all body types because if you don't have curves, it creates them, and if you do, it accentuates them nicely in an intentional way. The pencil skirt is a working woman's style staple. It helps craft a pulled-together and professional look that is still feminine. Finally, a full or flowing skirt rounds things out. Here, you can opt for a full mini (hits midthigh to knee), a full midi (falls between the knee and the calf), or a maxi (which should sweep the floor).

The easiest way to style a skirt for a casual outing is to pair it with a tee and flat shoes (either ankle boots or sandals). For a dressed-up look, a tucked-in blouse with a belt, heels, and a blazer is a classic choice.

SKIRTS

WHO TO SHOP	INTEGRITY RATING	DIAMOND LEVEL	PRICE
Amour Vert	organic, local	eco-warrior	$$
Samantha Pleet	natural (sustainable) fibers, local	eco-warrior	$$$
H Fredriksson	natural fibers, local	eco-warrior	$$$
Ace & Jig	natural fibers, social	eco-warrior	$$
Mahiya (by Free People)	natural fibers, social	eco-warrior	$$

Dressed-Up Dresses

Whether you are going on a first date or interviewing for a new job, the dress is a safe and stylish choice. There are many options, so the best thing to do is determine which styles and cuts look best on you. For instance, my legs are my pride and joy, so I typically opt for shorter lengths on the bottom with a more covered-up top to balance things out. Your environment may also play an influencing factor in your choice. Colder weather is perfect for sweater dresses, whereas a hot night out in the city calls for a breathable sheath.

And, of course, there is the tried-and-true little black dress (LBD). Every woman should own at least one of these that fits perfectly and makes her feel like a million bucks! This is one area where price holds no influence. The right LBD for you could be $40 or $400, so don't get caught up in what you think it should look like or cost. Be open to trying different styles at different price points, and sure enough, you will find one that will be with you for decades, ready for just about any occasion you throw it into. That is the beauty of the LBD. The simplicity of the LBD allows for eccentric and personal embellishments to be added to your overall look in the form of statement jewelry or a fantastic pair of heels. Those finishing touches are how you communicate your personal style and allow you to change your look continually without investing in a new dress each time.

DRESSES

WHO TO SHOP	INTEGRITY RATING	DIAMOND LEVEL	PRICE
David Peck	local, natural fibers, organic, social	eco-guru	$$$$
Titania Inglis	natural fibers, local, organic, veg dyes, upcycled	eco-guru	$$$$
Suzanne Rae	natural fibers, local	eco-warrior	$$$$
Obakki	social, local	eco-warrior	$$$
Isoude	natural fibers, local	eco-warrior	$$$$

Style Secret: To create smooth lines and a streamlined appearance, use proper undergarments that can help contour, hold in, and push up all the (ahem) right places. At the time of this writing eco-underwear options are still pretty limited, so my suggestion is to invest in quality undergarments from Wolford and Spanx until there are suitable eco-alternatives. That way, you know your purchases will deliver what's needed and last for years.

ACCESSORIES

By far, accessories are the easiest way to spruce up an outfit and update one's wardrobe. We've already talked about shoes (shoe lover that I am, I could not resist giving them their own section), and there are other key accessories that contribute to your signature style and overall aesthetic, such as handbags, jewelry, sunglasses, hats, gloves, and scarves.

The important thing to remember about accessories is that they will be with you for decades, so invest in quality. The only exception is with jewelry. There is a place and time for expensive (perhaps even family heirloom) jewelry, but you can also get away with wearing costume jewelry that is relatively inexpensive, bold, and very fun. I would also say that if you are notorious for losing jewelry (we all know who we are), save yourself the stress of worrying over a lost piece of expensive jewelry (or even sunglasses, if you leave those all the time too) and stick with the more affordable versions that are easy to replace and don't hold sentimental value.

Green Guide: The rule for accessories is quality over quantity. It is far better to spend a little more on higher standard materials and assembly. Accessories become your personalization beacons and have the longest life out of all the items in your closet. You may need to spend more upfront, but when you break it down into the cost per wear analysis, you'll find it well worth it.

When shopping for a handbag, the criteria I introduced in the shoe section on whether to go with leather or a vegan alternative also applies. My personal beef (no pun intended) with vegan bags is that the quality (at the moment) is usually inferior to their leather counterparts. I have sported vegan bags only to have them bleed their color onto my pants and white electronics, fall apart at the seams (literally!), and, in general, age disastrously like the overtanned and crinkled old woman in *There's Something About Mary*. To me, that is not a smart investment.

That said, I eat a macrobiotic diet that is pretty much vegan (except the occasional egg or piece of fish), and I have a real love for animals and their quality of life. So to appease both my stylish pragmatic side and my sensitive animal-loving side, I seek out brands that use leather and hides that are byproducts of the meat industry (until the world shifts to eating less or no meat, we might as well honor the life taken and use all of the animal). I also look for lines that use discarded leather and upcycle it into stylish accessories like bags, wallets, belts, and gloves. Again, if the leather is vegetable tanned, it is even better. Throw in some local production, and we are operating at the eco-guru level!

Jewelry is one of the best areas to shop while supporting a cause. There are so many women's cooperatives set up around the world that either utilize an indigenous or learned skill to produce some really beautiful pieces. When you shop these lines you support those co-ops and the local economy around them. In addition, bigger brands will often tap into jewelry production to raise funds for an organization or to aid disaster relief. As a consumer, you get the best of both worlds: a stylish piece for your wardrobe and an opportunity to support a cause.

Another ethical jewelry alternative is to shop brands that use upcycled materials like leather, metal, beads, and gems. Finally, if you are making an investment in precious jewelry, start with secondhand or vintage pieces. Like a nice wine, they get better with time and likely have a beautiful backstory. If you are set on new jewelry, just make sure that it is sourced ethically and through fair trade standards. Many brands have shifted their production to include recycled metal and ensure that their diamonds are not blood diamonds, but do your homework (check out their website and Google for any news articles on that brand) to be sure.

Shopping for sunglasses (or eyewear) is a lot like shopping for jewelry. You can find brands that are linked to social causes, like TOMS and Warby Parker. You can also find sunnies that are made from more sustainable materials like bamboo and recycled metals. Whichever you choose, just make sure they offer complete UVA/UVB protection. You can, of course, go the vintage route here too and find some great classic shapes made from quality materials.

The best eco-conscious way for bringing hats into your wardrobe is either to shop secondhand or to look for brands made locally using natural fibers.

Gloves fall under the vegan and pleather debate as well, but because they are small, it is easier to find upcycled versions. You can also opt for knit gloves and hand warmers that are made locally using ethical or upcycled yarn that is either untreated or vegetable dyed.

Scarves are my weakness (second to shoes!). They are the ultimate way of bringing a dash of color and personality into your overall look. Because they are so versatile (one size fits all), they are an ideal choice for socially linked brands. There are endless options in this category where the scarves are made by women in Ghana, Ireland, or North Carolina—and all with a sustainable economic impact. My go-to criteria in this area is to look for natural fiber use and a link to a cause or community.

Handbags

Beyond their sheer usefulness (where else can you store your phone, Kindle, wallet, lipstick, brush, keys, and sunglasses while you carry them with you?), the handbag is a beautiful indicator of your personal style. The "It Bag" trend will come and go, but the consciously minded fashionista knows that they are neither economically nor environmentally beneficial. You really only need about four different styles of bags: a structured tote, a cross-body satchel, an everyday shoulder bag, and an evening bag or clutch.

The tote is best for traveling and the office. The satchel is a more laid-back option that does nicely on the weekends and when you are touring around a city sightseeing. The shoulder bag can also be in the style of a bowler bag and be worn on the forearm instead off the shoulder. What you are really after is something smaller than a tote, and this is a perfect opportunity to purchase an investment bag, as it is the bag you'll carry almost every day. The evening bag can be a smaller pouch attached to a cross-body chain strap, an oversized clutch, or a bejeweled handheld box, each of which is appropriate for different events.

If you are unsure what kind of bag you'd like to incorporate into your wardrobe, keep an eye out when you walk the streets, look for them in movies on characters you relate to, and peruse magazines and style blogs to see which bags women you find to be inspiring are carrying. Below are some suggestions for handbag shopping. They include brands that uphold the green criteria I mentioned above. Also, a quality designer bag *really* will stand the test of time, so don't shy away from shopping upscale resale to get one, especially if you find that a designer bag better aligns with your style identity.

HANDBAGS

WHO TO SHOP	INTEGRITY RATING	DIAMOND LEVEL	PRICE
Cornelia Guest	vegan	eco-citizen	$$$
Stella McCartney	vegan	eco-citizen	$$$$
Gunas	vegan	eco-citizen	$$$
Calleen Cordero	veg tanned, local	eco-warrior	$$$$
The Sway NYC	upcycled	eco-citizen	$$$

Style Secret: If your wardrobe is made up mostly of neutrals (and lots of black), go for a colored or print bag to liven up your look. I love a burnt orange or "snakeskin"-style bag! Conversely, if your closet is full of bright and bold pieces, opt for a classic bag in a neutral color that goes with everything (black or brown).

Jewelry

Jewelry is a very personal expression of your style, so I am not going to tell you what you should or should not wear. I will say, however, that there are some staples that most women find useful when completing a look, and I've included those here for any of you who don't know where to start. Fill your jewelry box with these staples: a statement necklace (or two—I like to layer them for real drama), one or two metal or wood cuff bracelets, a fabulous eye-catching cocktail ring, a string of pearls, diamond stud earrings, statement earrings that dangle, an assortment of dainty metal and cloth-braided bracelets that you can layer and wear all at once, a special pendant necklace, and a watch.

JEWELRY

WHO TO SHOP	INTEGRITY RATING	DIAMOND LEVEL	PRICE
Dirty Librarian Chains	upcycled, local	eco-warrior	$$
by Natalie Frigo	local, upcycled	eco-warrior	$$$
Lizzie Fortunato Jewels	upcycled	eco-citizen	$$$
Muses & Rebels	local	eco-citizen	$$
Maiden Nation	social, upcycled	eco-warrior	$

Style Secret: Coco Chanel famously said that a woman should get ready to go, and then just before stepping out the door take one thing off. In other words, don't pile it all on at once. As a general rule, if you are wearing a statement necklace, you should leave the earrings off. Or if you are wearing a couple of metal bracelets, bring out your big drop earrings to finish off the look.

Eyewear

It is amazing how much of a cool factor a pair of sunnies can lend, but it is true. Additionally, the right pair of spectacles communicates your personal style across all outfits. Sunglasses are the cash cow of the fashion industry. Every season a new style comes out and becomes the must-have pair. Yet time has told a different story, and if you invest in just three styles, you'll be covered. Pick up a pair of aviators, wayfarers, and oversized sunglasses, and you are set for all occasions and outfits.

EYEWEAR

WHO TO SHOP	INTEGRITY RATING	DIAMOND LEVEL	PRICE
Warby Parker	social	eco-citizen	$$
TOMS Eyewear	social	eco-citizen	$$
Eco Optics by MODO	recycled, social	eco-warrior	$$$
Gucci (liquid wood line)	natural (sustainable) materials	eco-citizen	$$$
ICU Eyewear	recycled/upcycled	eco-citizen	$

Style Secret: To find the perfect pair of eyewear frames, scour magazines and iconic actresses from films from which you responded to their eyewear choice and style to establish a starting place. Then clue a stylish and honest friend in on what you are looking for. Take them with you to try on frames and let them choose for you. Sometimes we are too stuck in our own minds to see what actually flatters our face most.

Hats

Some people are hat people, and every style looks great on them. Others need to more accurately seek out the right fit and style for their head shape. Regardless, hats can add quite a lot to any outfit and are your best defense against the harsh rays of the sun, so they are worth having around. On a functional level I carry a visor in my bag so that if I am out to lunch and sitting in the sun, I can comfortably pop it on and enjoy my lunch and visit with my friend without worrying that my face is getting too much sun. The more stylish options include the fedora (straw and felt), a wide-rimmed sun hat (usually made from straw or canvas), a baseball cap or trucker hat (these come in and out of trend as a Hollywood staple and can actually be a good option while traveling to help out on a bad hair day), cowboy hats (pretty much reserved for certain parts of the country), and beanies. Knit beanies are gaining momentum in the eco-fashion space because of their materials (ethical, vegetable-dyed wool or cashmere) and the easy production that can be outsourced to communities in developing nations to help them gain economic stability (check out KrochetKids.org).

HATS

WHO TO SHOP	INTEGRITY RATING	DIAMOND LEVEL	PRICE
Live Worldly	natural fibers, social	eco-warrior	$
Valdez	natural fibers, social	eco-warrior	$$
Fair+True	fair trade, social, natural fibers	eco-guru	$
Pachacuti	fair trade, natural fibers, transparent	eco-guru	$$
Krochet Kids	social, fair trade	eco-warrior	$

Style Secret: If you haven't washed your hair for a couple of days, touch up the ends with a curling iron to create some loose waves, and then pop on a hat. This is a great time saver in a pinch, and the result is a pulled-together and intentional look.

Gloves and Scarves

On a cold day these two pieces are not only the finishing touches to your outfit but also essential for keeping you warm. Beyond function, they can be quite fashionable, and I would advise you hold out on purchasing a pair of gloves or a warm scarf until you find the ones that really speak as extensions of your overall style. For example, I recently bought a pair of leather-studded driving gloves from a famous secondhand store in Tokyo. I know that they will add to my overall look and take my winter attire up a notch. Similarly, a beautiful, quality-made scarf can communicate that you are a woman who likes a bit of luxury in her life.

GLOVES AND SCARVES

WHO TO SHOP	INTEGRITY RATING	DIAMOND LEVEL	PRICE
Dents	local, upcycled	eco-warrior	$$
The North Circular	local, fair trade, natural fibers	eco-guru	$$
The Andean Collection	natural fibers, fair	eco-warrior	$$
Indigo Handloom	natural fibers, fair trade, veg dyes	eco-guru	$$
Jane Carr	local, natural fibers	eco-warrior	$$$$

Style Secret: Because scarves are nearest to your face, they are the ideal place to bring in a pop of color. Remember which colors best suit your color way, and try one in a complementing color. You'll be surprised at the way it makes your complexion glow!

Reading through this chapter, you may have realized that there are gaps in your closet and pieces you'd like to add. Use the space below to make a list. By being clear about what you need, you'll be able to construct a more balanced and working wardrobe.

ITEM	POTENTIAL BRANDS	INTEGRITY RATING	DIAMOND LEVEL

This chapter will help you get a handle on some of the essentials that help to build a sustainable wardrobe. Yet my recommendations are simply suggestions, and by referencing the Green Guides before you buy and taking your integrity factors and Diamond Diagram with you, the options are endless.

CHAPTER 6

STYLE SORTED, LADIES: INNERWEAR, OUTERWEAR, AND ACTIVEWEAR

"If you're wearing lingerie that makes you feel glamorous, you're halfway to turning heads."

—ELLE MACPHERSON

LINGERIE AND SLEEPWEAR

There is always a bit of a romantic fervor that surrounds shopping for what Elizabeth Gilbert coyly calls our "delicates." There's just something about beautifully made lingerie (or sleepwear, for that matter) that gives you a telepathic pep talk and transforms your mood. However, there is a balance to wearing the frilly and sexy stuff (the bedroom equals primetime) and where you need to be more practical and get the support and smooth, seamless lines from no-fuss intimates.

Lingerie and intimate apparel are all about fit. If you get the fit wrong, you will be doing your body a grave disservice. Luckily, it is easy to assess your assets properly with the help of trained professionals. If you visit any department store or specialty lingerie shop, they will have a fit specialist on hand. Let them guide you, because your preconceived ideas about what bra you should be wearing might be off. By a lot.

Green Guide: An obvious choice for innerwear is to opt for organic fabrics. Other sustainable fabrics like modal and Tencel are often blended with an organic cotton to create comfortable pieces that have a little natural stretch built in. Silk and peace silk (made from ethically harvested silkworms that are not killed in the process) are perfect for camisoles, slips, and negligees.

As with more body-conscious (body-con) skirts and dresses, underwear and bras call for a touch of elastic to help ensure a proper fit and comfort. The best thing you can do is look for innerwear that is mostly made from organic and sustainable fabrics and are vegetable dyed. These are the pieces you are wearing closest to your body, so their purity (free from pesticides and chemical dyes) is important. One final eco-option is to look for underwear that is made from the offcuts of other fashion production. Because of the smaller size and fabric use, underwear created from leftover pieces of standard garment production is an excellent way to reduce waste.

LINGERIE AND SLEEPWEAR

WHO TO SHOP	INTEGRITY RATING	DIAMOND LEVEL	PRICE
Clare Bare	natural (sustainable) fibers, local	eco-warrior	$$$
Stella McCartney	organic, recycled	eco-warrior	$$
Fred & Ginger	natural (sustainable) fibers, local	eco-warrior	$$$$
Lilipiache	natural fibers, local	eco-warrior	$$
Daisy & Elizabeth	organic, recycled, natural fibers, local	eco-guru	$$

BRAS AND UNDIES

WHO TO SHOP	INTEGRITY RATING	DIAMOND LEVEL	PRICE
Only Hearts	local, organic	eco-warrior	$$
Pact	organic, natural fibers, fair trade	eco-guru	$
Hanky Panky	local	eco-citizen	$$
Nico Underwear	local, fair trade, natural fibers	eco-guru	$
Blue Canoe	organic, local	eco-warrior	$

Style Secret: Save lacy bras for the bedroom, and make sure you have a nude, seamless T-shirt bra to wear under sheer and more form-fitting shirts. You'll also want to have a convertible strapless bra in your arsenal to help equip you for various neck and back lines.

HOSIERY

Nina Garcia, fashion director of *Marie Claire* magazine, listed black opaque tights as one of her one hundred fashion pieces every woman should own, and I absolutely agree. The opaque tight can never look vulgar or run the risk of being too sexy. It is a chic staple that also plays its role for warmth and style during cooler months. A modern-day woman also needs sheer nude-colored footies or knee-high stockings to wear under trousers with pumps or ballet flats during cold weather. They help keep your feet warm and drastically minimize rubbing and blisters.

Green Guide: Hosiery is a bit tricky on the green front. There are more brands now producing ethically and environmentally made socks, but tights are still hard to get. Stick to quality in this category, as something that lasts over time is really quite sustainable. And keep your eye out for new brands that do incorporate eco-standards. I am sure it is only a matter of time before there are a plethora of options.

HOSIERY

WHO TO SHOP	INTEGRITY RATING	DIAMOND LEVEL	PRICE
Zkano	organic, fair trade, local	eco-guru	$
Brooklyn Industries	recycled, local	eco-warrior	$
Greenfibres	organic	eco-citizen	$
Tightology	organic, local, recycled	eco-guru	$
Maggie's Organics	fair trade, natural fibers, organic	eco-guru	$

ACTIVEWEAR

Today, being active is such an integral part of our everyday lives that we'll often start the day with a morning yoga class and leave our flexible attire on half the day! I would encourage you to change out of your activewear, mostly because you will feel and look so much better if you make an effort to get dressed and join the rest of the world. (Don't worry, I have to motivate myself too—those Pilates pants are so comfortable!).

Get dressed for you, but also get dressed for the people around you whom you will be interacting with all day. This is a very French approach, but I think there is some real value that can be gained. An American writer who was living in France once wrote about a dinner party conversation in which the French persons at the table explained to her that they always get dressed properly and comb their hair before stepping out in the morning, even if just to pick up a loaf of bread for breakfast, because it is a courtesy to the baker to look nice; it is a way of showing respect to him and his business. I love thinking about getting dressed this way. What a wonderfully considerate approach! Bottom line: wear activewear when you are being active. The rest of the time put a bit more effort into your appearance.

Green Guide: Once again, because of the stretch factor, finding purely organic and natural fiber clothing is difficult (though garments made mostly from organic cotton are a great place to start). There will be a small percent of spandex added to help the clothes stretch and form to your body. I would advise looking for brands that sustainably produce active apparel. Puma has a very high, longstanding sustainability rating in relation to their manufacturing practices, so you can feel good about supporting a big brand that is committed to function, style, and sustainability. I would also look for brands that are using recycled materials. Nike Better World is a perfect example. They use discarded materials from previously used running shoes to create new ones and are working with Teijin to produce garments made from preconsumer recycled textiles. Of course, I probably don't need to tell you that Patagonia has been the leader in this space for the past few decades. They also use recycled textiles and upcycled PET to produce their clothing and offer a take-back program through which you can send in any garments that have worn out over time to have them repaired or replaced.

By and large the activewear space is leading the eco-apparel front. They have been innovating on a form and function level for years, so you will have plenty of options. Lastly, you can always shop resale stores that specialize in outdoor gear and apparel.

YOGA AND STUDIO WEAR

WHO TO SHOP	INTEGRITY RATING	DIAMOND LEVEL	PRICE
Wellicious	organic, natural fibers, social, local	eco-guru	$$
Gaiam	natural fibers, local, organic	eco-guru	$$
EKO (Earth Kind Originals)	organic, fair trade	eco-warrior	$$
Lululemon Athletica	fair trade, social	eco-warrior	$$
Alo	organic, natural fibers	eco-warrior	$$

OUTDOOR LAYERS

WHO TO SHOP	INTEGRITY RATING	DIAMOND LEVEL	PRICE
Patagonia	organic, recycled, social	eco-guru	$$$
Nau	recycled, social, natural fibers, organic	eco-guru	$$$
Nike	recycled, organic, social	eco-guru	$$
Timberland	recycled (select pieces)	eco-citizen	$$
Columbia	recycled (select pieces)	eco-citizen	$$

SNEAKERS

WHO TO SHOP	INTEGRITY RATING	DIAMOND LEVEL	PRICE
Nike	recycled, fair trade, social	eco-guru	$$
Puma	fair trade, recycled, transparent	eco-guru	$$
Saucony	vegan	eco-citizen	$$
Montrail	vegan	eco-citizen	$$
Brooks	vegan	eco-citizen	$$

OUTERWEAR

I feel like I have saved the best for last, because I am a little obsessed with jackets and coats. As I already mentioned, I dress according to the weather. Well, that is half of the story. I also put an outfit together based on what I think it will look like on the street. A fully planned ensemble, in which all the pieces work well together, is my ultimate kick. Just like accessories, a cropped blazer or knee-length overcoat can perfect an outfit by balancing proportions and help to create your desired overall look.

Green Guide: Whereas in other categories you can look to more mainstream brands that are incorporating eco-initiatives, I find that going straight to eco-fashion-focused designers for outerwear is the best bet. This area usually requires a bit more of an ethical commitment, and by going with an eco-designer to begin with, you ensure a more unique design as well as confirmation of the considered standards you hold near and dear.

Conversely, I will say that fast-fashion retailers are jumping on the eco-fashion band-wagon with increased enthusiasm all the time, and thus, their offerings are expanding. Both H&M (with their Conscious Collection, which uses organic cottons and recycled materials) and Mango (which boasts a Made in Green tag on the majority of their garments now) seasonally put out new cuts and styles for wardrobe basics like a fitted blazer, cropped jacket, or army green anorak. For these lighter layers, shopping major retailers with eco-creds is fine. I would recommend that you look to independent designers in the eco-fashion space for heavier outerwear and coats to make certain you are getting high-quality fabrics and manufacturing on a piece that will be with you for decades.

Jean Jackets, Anoraks, and Trenches

Every wardrobe needs one of each. A classic slim-fitting jean jacket helps bring a relaxed and casual feel to daytime and summer evening dresses. The anorak (I prefer army green, but metallics, burnt brown, and khaki are all great too) is the quintessential cover-up for a spring or fall day when the temperatures are still fluctuating. They look best with a pair of rolled jeans, loafers, and an easy tee. A trench coat is a wardrobe staple. The modern take on this classic is cropped and imparts a younger attitude and more casual feel. If you are only going to buy one, go for the original. The signature khaki color goes with everything. Also, be sure to select a style that hits at or slightly above your knee so you can wear it both with trousers and short dresses.

JEAN JACKETS, ANORAKS, AND TRENCHES

WHO TO SHOP	INTEGRITY RATING	DIAMOND LEVEL	PRICE
Edun	natural fibers, social	eco-warrior	$$$$
Organic by John Patrick	recycled, natural fibers, local, organic	eco-guru	$$$$
Covet	natural fibers, organic	eco-warrior	$$$
Burning Torch	local, recycled	eco-warrior	$$$$
Prairie Underground	local, natural fibers, organic	eco-guru	$$$

Style Secret: Make sure these lighter-weight layers are fitted, as they will help accentuate your shape instead of hiding you beneath them. Also, you can always add a belt around the outside to cinch things in.

Blazers and Cozies

During my years in London I learned the importance of the blazer. No other single item can add such polish and authority! Over the years designers have pushed the limits of the blazer, coming up with new cuts and styles that are more appropriate for certain outfits and occasions than are others. There are essentially three basic styles I would recommend you incorporate into your wardrobe: the classic-fit blazer, a cropped blazer, and the boyfriend (or smoking jacket) blazer. The classic blazer is best for formal occasions and pairs nicely with slim-leg trousers and pencil skirts. You can also pop it on over a T-shirt with a pair of jeans and driving shoes for a textbook weekend look. The cropped blazer helps balance out the proportions of a flowing maxi dress and also looks fab with a high-waisted and belted skirt or a knee-length body-con dress. The boyfriend blazer leans toward a more casual and cool look, in which you may pair a sequin top with a leather mini and add the boyfriend blazer to balance the glam factor.

The cozy is a modern-day take on the long cardigan and was made famous by Donna Karan, who first brought the shape to the marketplace. The cut is slightly higher in the back, and the front is left open with longer ends that dip down toward midthigh. Many consider the cozy to be the casual version of a blazer. It layers nicely over pretty much anything, and you can choose to leave it open and flowing or rein it in with a belt. They are absolutely perfect for traveling because they provide warmth and style.

BLAZERS AND COZIES

WHO TO SHOP	INTEGRITY RATING	DIAMOND LEVEL	PRICE
Eileen Fisher	fair trade, recycled	eco-warrior	$$$
Heidi Merrick	local, vegan	eco-warrior	$$$$
Kami Organic	organic, natural fibers	eco-warrior	$$$$
NearFar	natural fibers, fair trade, social	eco-guru	$$
DKNY Pure	natural fibers	eco-citizen	$$$

Leather Jackets

Nothing spells cool like a leather jacket. Of course, the leather versus pleather debate is applicable here too (you can see my thoughts on the matter in Chapter 2). Whether you decide on a real or faux option, vintage and secondhand shops are a great starting place. Real leather gets better over time, so you can often find a real gem that is already broken in for you. Alternatively, eco-focused designers are notorious for creating stylish numbers from upcycled leather and byproduct leather from the meat industry.

When I am in New York I basically live in my leather jacket from the Sway NYC. Over a tank with a pair of boyfriend jeans or with a structured dress and heels—it is the optimal choice for a casual cool look.

LEATHER JACKETS

WHO TO SHOP	INTEGRITY RATING	DIAMOND LEVEL	PRICE
Holmes & Yang	local, natural fibers	eco-warrior	$$$$
The Sway NYC	upcycled, fair trade	eco-warrior	$$$$
Free People	vegan	eco-citizen	$$$
Thu Thu	local, fair trade, veg dyes	eco-guru	$$$$
The Reformation	recycled, local	eco-warrior	$$$

Style Secret: You don't have to stick with black for a leather jacket. Brown, gray, and tan won't look as dressy as black, but depending on where you wear it, that might be ideal.

Winter Coats and Vests (Down and Faux Fur)

Growing up in Wyoming, winters conditioned me to be ever appreciative of a warm coat. The goal with purchasing a winter coat is to find something that reflects the environment around you, including the aesthetics and temperatures. For instance, if you live in an urban setting or city, you'll want a coat that shows off a designer cut and typically has more dressed-up details. Those of you who spend your time in the country or suburbs will need a coat that is more casual and approachable. I like to have both options, because I am often going between big cities and my hometown, where things are much more laid back than in Tokyo!

Both wool and puffy coats work well in the urban and rural setting, and having one of each gives you options. A down style or faux fur vest is another nice layer to have. On cool days when the sun peeks out, they are just right. For the most part you only need one down vest, but I like to recommend that younger gals who live in the city also invest in a faux fur (or vintage real fur) vest. The vest is the perfect piece to pop on while running errands or meeting friends for brunch.

WINTER COATS AND VESTS

WHO TO SHOP	INTEGRITY RATING	DIAMOND LEVEL	PRICE
White Tent	social, local, natural fibers	eco-guru	$$$
Vaute Couture	local, vegan, recycled	eco-guru	$$$$
Nanette Lepore	local, fair trade	eco-warrior	$$$$
Isabell de Hillerin	local, fair trade, natural fibers	eco-guru	$$$$
H Fredriksson	organic, natural fibers, local	eco-guru	$$$

By now you should feel you have a good grasp on what you need to build a balanced and accommodating wardrobe. Don't feel pressure to go out and fill any gaps you identified all at once. Part of the fun of building a wardrobe (and your personal style) is finding the perfect pieces over time. Use the space on the next page to jot down any items you discovered are missing from your wardrobe. Keep that list in mind as you travel, browse online, or head out on a shopping date with girlfriends.

STYLE SORTED, LADIES: INNERWEAR, OUTERWEAR, AND ACTIVEWEAR

ITEM	POTENTIAL BRANDS	INTEGRITY RATING	DIAMOND LEVEL

CHAPTER 7

STYLE SORTED, LADIES: SPECIAL OCCASIONS AND TRAVEL

"I think that playing dress-up begins at age five and never truly ends."

— KATE SPADE

It has taken me some time to admit it fully, but I am a girly girl. I suppose my first clue would have been from when I was eight years old and wearing dresses and lipstick to bed so I could look my best for school the next day. Okay, you might as well call me a princess with a story like that, but I honestly don't know a single woman who does not like to dress up now and then. It is our chance to indulge, pamper, and shine. So when the invitation calls for a semiformal or formal dress code, embrace the opportunity to play dress-up.

Green Guide: There are a few ways you can go green in this department. One option is to invest in a high-quality cocktail dress and a long evening gown in a dark, solid color (black is best, but a dark blue or purple can also work well). That way you can wear them over and over again for various occasions, changing your accessories to change your look. For some women this an ideal solution; for others, variety is key. Here you have a couple of choices: you can shop vintage or secondhand and alter pieces to give them your own spin, or you can rent. Vintage gowns are making quite the comeback on the red carpet, as more and more celebs take the Green Carpet Challenge (created by Livia

Firth). If you have an affinity for classic shapes and styles from the past, this is a great way to go. Just be sure to leave time for alterations to ensure a proper fit.

Renting dresses, both vintage and new, has really gained momentum and is an economically chic option. Lastly, there are eco-fashion designers who specialize in creating glamorous gowns and party dresses made locally, ethically, and using recycled material or natural (sustainable) fibers. If you are looking to add some permanent options to your closet, this is a great way to go.

COCKTAIL PARTIES AND FUNDRAISERS

Attire for cocktail parties and fundraisers is fairly similar, though the fundraiser outfit will likely run a more conservative track. Even if the cocktail party is more casual, you'll want to dress up a little to show respect for your hosts. Go for a form-fitting dress with a modest neckline, and add some statement jewelry. Or try out a three-quarter-length sequin top with slim black cigarette pants and a pair of pointed-toe heels.

BIRTHDAYS AND NEW YEAR'S EVE

Your birthday and NYE present the perfect occasions to break all the rules and go for glamour with a side of drama! If you want to sparkle, load on the sequins and metallic accessories. If there is a new trend you'd like to try, now is the time. The fun-filled energy that surrounds both of these occasions is light and airy, so take advantage. Opt for something that lets you feel sexy and confident. That may be an embellished LBD, a sequin mini, or a pair of leather pants. Add shine and shimmer with key accessories, and don't be afraid to be more heavy-handed with your makeup. And always wear heels.

Style Secret: If you are attending a B-day bash, don't outshine the birthday girl, but do keep your outfit on par with the occasion.

BLACK TIE EVENTS AND THE OPERA

Whereas attending the symphony and theater performances usually warrant a cocktail party–type outfit, the opera and any invitation that specifically states the dress code as black tie require a gown. In the winter choose heavier fabrics like velvet and wool. During the summer opt for chiffons and silks in brighter hues and prints. Regardless of the season, you'll need to include some statement jewelry that catches the eye (costume or real), like a set of gorgeous drop earrings or a defining necklace. Closed-toe pumps and wedges won't work for this outfit; instead, go for a strappy-heeled sandal or a D'Orsay-style peep-toe pump. Finish off your outfit with a cropped cape and a handheld clutch.

Style Secret: Get a blow-out the day of your event. Full hair helps balance out a floor-length dress.

WEDDINGS

Weddings are my absolute favorite! Everyone is gushing with love and ready to get down and celebrate. Some brides are very particular about the theme and feel of their wedding and will want their guests to dress accordingly. If you get this sense and they haven't provided attire guidelines, ask for more direction. Stay away from white, beige, and ivory; you don't want to be that woman competing with the bride. Some weddings are more casual and call for cocktail attire, whereas others are distinctly more formal.

If the wedding takes place during the day, lighten your look. You can easily do this with a day dress that hits at the knee and isn't made from a luxe fabric like satin or velvet. Opting for bright, happy colors and floral prints is great too. You can wear a maxi-style dress, so long as it has more of a daytime, relaxed feel. Add a belt, turquoise jewelry, and wedges to keep the overall outfit more relaxed.

If you attend a wedding where the ceremony begins in the late afternoon and the party rolls out afterward and runs until midnight, go for a more dressed-up look. Again, I would highly recommend renting a dress from RentTheRunway.com. With each rental they allow you to rent a second style for a little extra. I will rent the dress I plan on wearing the day of the wedding and use my second style to get a dress for the rehearsal dinner the night before. Speaking of rehearsal dinners, dress like you are going to a cocktail party. Wear something classy and festive. If it is more relaxed, think of it as a garden cocktail party.

DRESSED-UP DRESSES

WHO TO SHOP	INTEGRITY RATING	DIAMOND LEVEL	PRICE
David Peck	organic, local, social, natural fibers	eco-guru	$$$$
100% NY	organic, local, upcycled, natural fibers	eco-guru	$$$
Minna	recycled, zero waste, natural fibers, local	eco-guru	$$$
Ada Zanditon	natural fibers, organic, fair trade, AZO-free dyes	eco-guru	$$$$
Allison Parris	local, natural fibers, upcycled	eco-guru	$$$

TRAVEL

Traveling is exciting and fun, but when you don't know what to pack, that fun-filled attitude can turn to stress. I've become a seasoned traveler and have been lucky enough to visit many countries and climates, and along the way I have figured out some packing essentials that will make both prepping for and enjoying your final destination a joy.

The first thing to do is check the weather for where you are headed (no surprise there!). If you are traveling between seasons, pack a warmer jacket and even a beanie just in case global warming has screwed up the weather and you find yourself a victim of our new crazy weather patterns. I also keep a travel-size umbrella stored in the bottom of my suitcase.

What to Pack: Ski Holiday

Whether you plan to shred all day or lounge slope-side, you'll need some go-to pieces to keep you warm and stylish for a winter holiday. Leggings are at the top of my list, though you always want to pair them with a top that is long enough to cover your bum. Jeans are also key. Pair with a cashmere hoodie, a puffer vest, and snow boots for the modern take on a well-dressed snow bunny. Sweater dresses were made for winter dinner parties and can be dressed up with earrings and a pair of riding boots. I also love a beautiful cashmere shawl; when you take an afternoon off and read by the fire, there is nothing better.

Heading to the mountains? Here's my packing list:

- leggings
- sweater dress x 2
- dark-wash jeans (one pair)
- thermal underwear (top and bottom)
- scarves (wool and cashmere, in beige, black, and a deep, rich color)
- snow boots
- midcalf wedge boots
- oversized sweater
- long cashmere hoodie
- long fitted tank or tee (under layers) x 2
- thick socks
- ski hat
- sunglasses
- sunblock
- gloves (for the mountain and around town)
- goggles
- ski apparel (pants and jacket)
- warm winter coat
- puffy quilted or faux fur vest
- swimsuit for the hot tub!

Style Secret: Remember to pop on a scarf or a vest to add a little more interest and warmth to your outfits.

SKI APPAREL

WHO TO SHOP	INTEGRITY RATING	DIAMOND LEVEL	PRICE
NWT3K	local (and customizable!)	eco-citizen	$$$
Patagonia	organic, recycled, social, fair trade	eco-guru	$$$
Klättermusen	organic, veg dyes	eco-warrior	$$$$
Nau	organic, natural fibers, recycled	eco-guru	$$$
Kjus	fair trade	eco-citizen	$$$$

APRÈS SKI APPAREL

WHO TO SHOP	INTEGRITY RATING	DIAMOND LEVEL	PRICE
Bamford	organic, natural fibers, fair trade	eco-guru	$$$
People Tree	fair trade, social, natural fibers	eco-guru	$$
Gudrun & Gudrun	organic, natural fibers, veg dyes	eco-guru	$$$
VOZ	fair trade, natural fibers	eco-warrior	$$$
Chinti and Parker	organic, fair trade	eco-warrior	$$

What to Pack: Swim Holiday

Heading to warmer weather makes packing that much easier. All you really need are a few swimsuits, some cover-ups, a sun hat, and a good book. Though tropical holidays are typically more laid back, it is important to know the dress code for any resort you might be staying at. Although resorts rarely enforce a dress code, you will feel better if you've brought some options that are conducive to the environment. Check with your reservations person ahead of time, and when in doubt bring a couple of nicer options so you can easily go to dinner without feeling like you should have stayed in and ordered room service.

Beach bound? Here's what to pack:

- cover-up x 3
- pair of cut-off shorts
- pair of tailored shorts
- tunic top (in silk, linen, or cotton)
- classic button-down (in white, powder blue, or chambray denim)
- basic tee x 2
- basic tank x 2
- swimsuits (I like to bring one for every day, but you really only need two or three)
- day dress x 3 (two short, one long)
- boyfriend cardi or zippered hoodie

- pair of flip-flops
- pair of fancy flat sandals
- pair of wedges
- canvas beach bag
- sun hat
- sunglasses
- sunblock (face and body)
- sarong/lightweight scarf
- statement earrings (turquoise is my go-to)
- long necklace (bring a few so you can layer them)

SWIMSUITS

WHO TO SHOP	INTEGRITY RATING	DIAMOND LEVEL	PRICE
Olga Olsson	social, fair trade	eco-warrior	$$
Cala Ossidiana	fair trade, local	eco-warrior	$$$
Faherty Brand	recycled	eco-citizen	$$
Odina Surf	recycled, local, social	eco-guru	$$
Greenlee Swim	recycled, local	eco-warrior	$$

COVER-UPS AND DAY DRESSES

WHO TO SHOP	INTEGRITY RATING	DIAMOND LEVEL	PRICE
LemLem	social, natural fibers	eco-warrior	$$
Lalesso	social	eco-citizen	$$
TWO	local, natural fibers, social	eco-guru	$$$$
Mizungu Sisters	social	eco-citizen	$$
Beach Candy	natural fibers, social	eco-warrior	$$

What to Wear on the Plane

One last piece of the traveling equation is figuring out what to wear on the plane. A lot of times you are coming from the climate that is in direct opposition to where you are going. The trick is to layer so that when you get there you can peel off layers or pile them on. My foolproof outfit goes something like this:

- tank
- semisheer white button-down
- skinny jeans
- fitted jacket
- quilted puffer vest

- ballet flats or sneakers (for warm-weather destinations) or ankle boots with socks (for snow)
- stacked bracelets
- a colorful scarf
- large carry-all tote

Obviously, in cool weather you will wear all of the layers. When you get to warm weather you can shed everything down to the tank, roll your jeans, and go sockless with your sneakers for a casual cool look. If you are headed to very cold weather, you will also want to carry on a proper winter coat and a hat.

With the wardrobe suggestions in this chapter and the previous two, your closet is complete. Again, half the fun is the time and experiences it takes to cultivate a well-curated wardrobe. Take your time. By using your Diamond Diagram, over time your wardrobe will help change the world as well as your evolved style.

CHAPTER 8

STYLE SORTED, GENTLEMEN

"A man should look as if he had bought his clothes with intelligence, put them on with care, and then forgotten all about them."

—HARDY AMIES

Easing into our clothes as though they are a second skin is what truly effortless style is all about. I am often so jealous of the way men are able to do just that! One may think that the options for men are pared down, and to some extent they are. However, men have so many wonderful accessories that subtly signify the kind of man they are and create a silent understanding and tribal code among them. If you are a woman reading this book, this chapter will serve as a guide to gift buying for the men in your life. If you are a guy, this chapter is just for you!

Gentlemen, I am going to assume that you have a self-professed interest in how you dress (likely part of the reason you're reading this book). Therefore, I am not going to waste precious pages convincing you that what you wear and how you wear it matter, that clothes are a language through which we instantly communicate with others to tell them who we are and what we think of ourselves. You already know that.

Whether you are a *Mad Men* enthusiast, laid-back hipster, color-coordinated dandy, balanced metrosexual, or something in between, there are style staples that will make the daily task of getting dressed that much easier and more fulfilling. Although I make suggestions in the following categories, they are just suggestions. I'm sure an internal nudge will tell you to try something or to discard it without a second thought. That is part of what makes your style uniquely yours. Yet bear in mind that sometimes we are stuck inside our own limiting thoughts, and a new cut or style can open our world and self-expression. Couple these style suggestions with their corresponding green guides, and you are well on your way to openly communicating exactly who you are (values and style included) with a simple passing glance!

The wear-no-evil approach to life encompasses ethics, but it starts with style. If the shirt you buy supports organic farming and the use of low-impact dyes but the style or fit is off, the item won't accurately reflect your sense of style and best self. That shirt will become a place holder in your drawer and never have the chance to make a real difference. Alas, before we jump ahead to explore eco-clothing options, you'll need to know yourself better: how to dress for your body type, what signature pieces you need in order to create a worthy wardrobe, and how to pull it all together.

FIT

Proper fit is so very important. A lot of guys don't pay attention to their sizing and buy whatever fits off the rack. That is fine, but knowing your body type and how to dress it can be transformative. There are essentially five basic body types for men: short, tall, average, extra in the middle, and barrel chested. You're probably a combination of at least two of those. I hate to say it, but in dressing to disguise a tummy or appear taller, guys often butcher the process and wind up highlighting what they meant to downplay. Read through the following style suggestions to gain insight on how to best dress for your body.

Short

If you are on the shorter side (let's say five foot seven or shorter), your main goal is to lengthen what you've got. There are many ways to help yourself appear taller, and they have everything to do with proper fit and flattering cuts. To add length up top, go for button-downs with vertical stripes, unbuttoned polo shirts that show a longer neckline, and V-neck tees. With any button-downs, be sure to have them tailored to hit one or two inches below your pant waistband. Any longer than that, and it will look like you were playing in your dad's closet. When you are buying trousers and jeans, make sure the fit in the thigh and tush are right on, and don't worry about the extra leg length. You should have your pants hemmed perfectly to your height, allowing for a slight break at the bottom of the pant. For the most streamlined look keep things monochromatic. Dark shoes and matching belts always help the leg look longer. When you need to buy a suit, buy one from a retailer who specializes in short suits. The cut and proper proportions will wind up helping you look lanky like you never thought possible. Go for a two-button jacket with a slightly lower stance so that your torso comes off as being longer by showing more of your tie. As a general rule, when dressing up opt for monochromatic looks in navy, gray, or black with a subtle pinstripe for an extra lengthening touch.

Tall

If you were born with a tall stature, you probably consider yourself very lucky—except when you are trying to find clothes that fit. If you are over six foot four you'll likely need to shop at stores that specialize in tall men sizing. Between six foot and six foot four you'll still get away with shopping at regular shops and asking for the longer/bigger sizes. Buy shirts that fit in the sleeve length and have them tailored in to fit your body. Jackets should still cover your butt, and one with three buttons works best. Go for a cuff with your trousers to break the leg line, and have fun wearing shoes that are bright and differently colored from your trousers. Tall men can also wear turtlenecks and high-collared sweaters. Crew neck tees look best. Printed blazers and overcoats are also a fun indulgence that your body type can support.

Average

The standard American man is around five foot ten. If you are over five foot seven and below six foot, you fall into this category. The average man has the easiest time shopping of all. An ideal silhouette is to have broad shoulders and a narrow waist. You can create this by purchasing jackets and blazers that sit perfectly on your shoulders (the seam ends at the line where your shoulder naturally drops off). Suit jackets should have sleeves that cover the wrist but not the hand and allow for your dress shirt to poke out slightly at the end. Smoking or casual jackets can be longer in the sleeves, as you'll likely wear them with more casual undershirts like a sweater or tee. For formal attire always match your shoes and belt. Trousers should retain a slouchy break at the bottom of the pant leg for a more relaxed feel, and steer clear of cuffs.

Extra in the Middle

If you have a tummy, don't fret—a lot of men (and women!) do. The key to dressing your tummy is to balance out the proportions of your body by creating strong shoulders and wider legs. That way you come across looking stocky all over instead of pudgy in the middle. Buy boxy jackets in stiff fabrics like leather. They will help dictate the shape of your upper half, not your tummy. Avoid stripes of any kind in shirts and sweaters, and opt for sweaters that don't end in a wide waistband (which draws attention to your pooch). You'll likely wear your shirts untucked, so it is important that the fit is good. Tailor shirts to come in slightly around the middle of your torso with a straight line, and make sure they never fall below your crotch. Tapered trousers are your nemesis and you'll want to only own pleatless pants that fall straight and have a wide leg, including with jeans. A little extra material at the end of the leg break can help create more interest for the eye when observing the overall look—pulling the eye away from the middle—and thus works in your favor. Chunky shoes also help balance out your weight and keep proportions in line. Unbuttoned driving jackets, peacoats, and scarves tossed around the back of the neck with the tails falling forward on either side create long lines and a leaner look.

Barrel Chested

If you feel you fit into this category, you have a broad and perhaps protruding chest. I like to think of this as the He-Man body type! Having a strong and solid presence comes naturally, but you will need to balance your top half with the rest of your body. Wide-leg jeans and trousers are great, and you can get away with a straight-leg pant for more formal occasions. Go for a midrise if you also have a bit of a belly to help reign things in. Boxy jackets are your best friend, and you can get any number of them in various styles and fabrics so long as the shoulder structure is strong and fits correctly. A barrel-chested man can pull off plaids and gingham, so don't be afraid to try them in button-downs and blazers. Balance your outfits with shoes that have more of a substantial feel to them (nothing too streamlined or svelte).

Now that you know how to dress for success in regard to your build and stature, we can merge ethics with style. For each of the following categories you'll find style advice, a go-green guide that highlights overarching ways to look for and shop green in that sector, plus a top-five wear-no-evil list of brands and their integrity ratings. Use this next section to guide your purchasing behavior and reclaim your power as a consumer.

PRICE CHECK

Throughout this chapter use this key to gauge the
price point of any item easily.

$ - - - - - - - - - $0–$50

$$ - - - - - - - - $50–$150

$$$ - - - - - - - $150–$350

$$$$ - - - - - - $350+

TOPS

From T-shirts and polos to sweaters and button-downs, there are many options for putting an outfit together. What styles and colors your choose communicate your personal tastes. Even if you are a T-shirt-and-jeans kind of guy, there will be an occasion (or two) that call for a dress shirt or a sweater. The key to choosing tops that work for you is to select the colors that naturally speak to you and to create variety. So many men get stuck buying the same color (everything is gray or black), or they're afraid to take a chance on a new pattern or cut. Try to incorporate a few items that still feel like you but push you out of your casual comfort zone so that you have options when getting dressed.

Green Guide: When shopping for tops you'll find it easiest to shop for those made from natural fibers, like organic cotton, linen, hemp, or even modal (made from beech wood pulp). Alternatively, there are loads of T-shirts being made from recycled PET. To up your eco-rating, look for items that use an air-dye process (textile dying technique that uses no water) or low-impact dyes that can carry the BlueSign certification seal. If you are adding some warmer layers to your wardrobe, again try to buy natural fibers like wool from ethically traced sources. So many brands are now sharing their sourcing stories in a transparent and documented way so that you know the whole process behind your purchase, from the sheep to the sewer.

T-SHIRTS

WHO TO SHOP	INTEGRITY RATING	DIAMOND LEVEL	PRICE
Pickwick & Weller	local, natural fibers, organic, fair trade	eco-guru	$
Mack Weldon	natural fibers	eco-citizen	$
Rogan	local, fair trade, natural fibers, organic	eco-guru	$$
Everlane	local, natural fibers	eco-warrior	$
Rag & Bone	local, natural fibers	eco-warrior	$$$

BUTTON-DOWNS

WHO TO SHOP	INTEGRITY RATING	DIAMOND LEVEL	PRICE
Thom Browne	local, natural fibers	eco-warrior	$$$
Seawall	natural fibers, fair trade, local	eco-guru	$$$
Hamilton Shirts	local, natural fibers	eco-warrior	$$$
Gitman Brothers	local, natural fibers	eco-warrior	$$$
Post Overalls	local, natural fibers	eco-warrior	$$$

SWEATERS AND CARDIGANS

WHO TO SHOP	INTEGRITY RATING	DIAMOND LEVEL	PRICE
Ramblers Way	local, natural fibers, organic, fair trade	eco-guru	$$$$
Band of Outsiders	natural fibers, local	eco-warrior	$$$$
Pendleton	local, fair trade, natural fibers	eco-guru	$$
Everlane	local, natural fibers	eco-warrior	$
SNS Herring	fair trade, natural fibers	eco-warrior	$$$

BOTTOMS

Today, jeans are a daily standard for men and women alike. However, having other options in a straight-leg style is key to dressing a tad more formally, which may be more appropriate for certain settings and occasions. For casual settings lightweight trousers are great, and you might even opt for a pair of shorts on a hot day.

Green Guide: Because jeans are mostly made from cotton, try to buy jeans made from organic or recycled cotton. There are also jeans that use much less water than the standard pair (which uses fifteen hundred gallons!), from Levi's Water<Less line and Jeanopia. Another option is to purchase pants made from recycled materials. You can also look for jeans made here in the US of A, like those from Jean Shop in New York City, who proudly boasts that all their jeans are made locally. For other trousers, like cords or chinos, look for brands that manufacture responsibly by linking their production to supporting local communities and transparent supply chains. One of my favorites in this area is the IOU Project, which uses hand-woven madras fabric for their signature colorfully checked trousers and shorts. Finally, shop locally. Support independent designers who produce their wares in the country you live in.

JEANS AND TROUSERS

WHO TO SHOP	INTEGRITY RATING	DIAMOND LEVEL	PRICE
IOU Project	transparent, fair trade, natural fibers	eco-guru	$$
Levi's Water<Less	water footprint	eco-citizen	$$
Edun	social, natural fibers	eco-warrior	$$$
Raleigh Denim	local, fair trade	eco-warrior	$$
3x1 Denim	local, organic, natural fibers, fair trade	eco-guru	$$$$

ACCESSORIES

A rare vintage watch or a monogrammed wallet—these subtle accessories define personal style for men. Some men can be quite showy in their fashion choices, with pieces that shout their point of view from head to toe. Others like to keep their fashion taste on the down low, revealing hints of extended effort in key accessories that were either gifts or hand selected. An on-trend pair of sunglasses, bright socks, or even a perfectly chosen murse (man purse) bring the whole look together.

Green Guide: Accessories present the perfect time to look for secondhand or vintage pieces. There is just so much out there already! Sunglasses from the 1970s inevitably make their way back into fashion. A classic timepiece that is handed down through a family is an honorable keepsake. But even ties and bowties are plentiful in thrift stores and can be adapted to modern-day styles (use the service from SkinnyFatties.com to update your ties). There is a lot of upcycling happening in the accessories space too. Items that were originally used as parachutes, army duffle bags, or even tires are being made into fashionable wallets, daily carry-alls, and iPad cases. Because accessories are a "one size fits all" gig, many brands like to link accessories to benefiting a cause, so that is one more way you can get in on the eco-initiatives in this category.

WALLETS AND BAGS

WHO TO SHOP	INTEGRITY RATING	DIAMOND LEVEL	PRICE
UNA	fair trade, social, natural fibers, organic	eco-guru	$$$
TM1985	upcycled, local, natural fibers	eco-guru	$$
Killspencer	local	eco-citizen	$$$$
Ernest Alexander	local	eco-citizen	$$$$
Joshu+Vela	local	eco-citizen	$$$

HAT, GLOVES, AND SCARVES

WHO TO SHOP	INTEGRITY RATING	DIAMOND LEVEL	PRICE
The North Circular	local, natural fibers, organic, fair trade	eco-guru	$$$
Dents	natural fibers, fair trade, local, upcycled	eco-guru	$$$
A.P.C.	natural fibers	eco-citizen	$$
Eugenia Kim's Mr. Kim	natural fibers	eco-citizen	$$$
Krochet Kids	social, fair trade	eco-warrior	$$

GLASSES, BELTS, AND TIES

WHO TO SHOP	INTEGRITY RATING	DIAMOND LEVEL	PRICE
Warby Parker	fair trade, social	eco-warrior	$$
Corter Leather & Cloth	veg tanned, local	eco-warrior	$$
David Hart & Co.	local, natural fibers	eco-warrior	$$
Westward Leaning	local	eco-citizen	$$$
General Knot & Co.	local, natural fibers .	eco-warrior	$$

SHOES

They say you don't know a man until you walk a mile in his shoes. These days you can tell quite a lot about a man just by the shoes he wears. From laid-back sneakers to perfectly polished oxfords, men's footwear has become an integral piece to crafting one's overall look and communicating personal style. With just six pairs of shoes, you'll have options for every occasion and can grow your collection from there. I recommend each man have: flip-flops, athletic shoes, low-top sneakers, dress shoes, and a pair of boots.

Green Guide: When talking about shoes, it is hard not to get into the leather versus pleather debate. (Take a look at Chapter 2 to see a full breakdown on the pros and cons.) If you are a vegan or are very sensitive about the treatment of animals, then you will likely always go for nonleather shoes (check out MooShoes.com for vegan footwear). However, if the environmental impact of synthetics and PVC (used to produce leather alternatives) is your top concern, ethically produced and vegetable-tanned leather options might be a better fit for you. Also, technical developments in this category are making it possible to use recycled and upcycled materials as well as zero-waste design, like the Flyknit sneaker from Nike, which is knit from a single thread. Finally, eco-friendly rubber made from trees (instead of oil) is another hot industry development and an area to watch for more eco-alternatives.

SHOES

WHO TO SHOP	INTEGRITY RATING	DIAMOND LEVEL	PRICE
TOMS	social, vegan	eco-warrior	$
EKN Footwear	natural fibers	eco-citizen	$$$
Kuyban	natural fibers, fair trade	eco-warrior	$$$
Timberland (Earthkeepers Collection)	upcycled/recyled materials	eco-citizen	$$
Nike Better World	recycled, social	eco-warrior	$$

SOCKS, UNDERWEAR, AND SWIMWEAR

Under-armor for men is often overlooked, but more and more it has become mainstream and relevant. Today, a flash of hot pink or yellow from underneath a pant leg signifies style cred. The sock scene has utterly exploded and given way to playful and intentional design status. Luckily, the underwear department is also undergoing a revolution of sorts, and men's boxers have never been more technically advanced or comfortable.

Green Guide: Because underwear sits closest to your, ahem, prized packages, opting for organic and natural fibers is best. With synthetics you run the risk of irritation and, in some cases, toxic dyes that are used can emit cancer-causing particles. As a rule of thumb, you can think of dressing your private parts like dressing a newborn baby: you'd want the purest pieces possible. It is also getting easier to find Made in USA socks and underwear, so keep an eye out.

For swimwear look for brands that produce locally and use recycled or upcycled materials. A lot of brands are now using recycled PET to make trendy trunks.

BASICS AND SWIMWEAR

WHO TO SHOP	INTEGRITY RATING	DIAMOND LEVEL	PRICE
Isaora	local, fair trade	eco-warrior	$$$
Onia	fair trade	eco-citizen	$$
Flint & Tinder	local, natural fibers	eco-warrior	$
Charles Mark & Sons	social, fair trade	eco-warrior	$
Pact	organic, natural fibers, fair trade	eco-guru	$

JACKETS AND SUITS

I am not the first woman to say this, and I can confidently speak on behalf of womankind: nothing is sexier than a cleaned-up man in a well-cut and fitted suit. Whether you wear a suit five days a week or have a couple hanging in the closet for special occasions, every man needs at least one summer suit and one winter suit. The difference is in both the fabrics and color. As a general rule, you can get away with having one gray suit (for summer) and one dark navy or black suit (usually in a heavier material, like a wool-cashmere blend). The great part about suits is that once you have one or two that are tailored to fit you perfectly, you can use the jackets separately as blazers to wear with jeans or other dress pants for a more casual smart look.

Green Guide: A great suit or jacket is an investment. Don't be afraid to spend a good chunk upfront on a well-made or custom-tailored suit. The cost per wear evens out over time and amounts to pennies per wear over a lifetime. The best you can do in this category is to buy high-end fabrics that will hold up over time, and either buy off the rack from a smaller and independent designer who produces locally or work with your tailor or a specialized suit maker to custom craft a suit to your specifications. The other option is to rent formal attire when needed. Most men don't need a tux on a regular basis, so renting one is both an economical and environmental option. Lastly, shop secondhand. Suits made from the 1940s and 1950s from quality designer fashion houses that employed artisan workforces produced exceptional pieces that will last for decades to come. Scoop up one of these gems and have your tailor refit it to your measurements.

WHO TO SHOP	INTEGRITY RATING	DIAMOND LEVEL	PRICE
Paul Smith	natural fibers	eco-citizen	$$$$
Theory	local (check garment)	eco-citizen	$$$$
Taylor Stitch	natural fibers, local	eco-warrior	$$$$
People Tree	natural fibers, fair trade	eco-warrior	$$$
Steven Alan	local (check garment)	eco-citizen	$$$$

OUTERWEAR AND ACTIVEWEAR

Stylish and technical outerwear is where form and function meet. A classic rain jacket that you can don for navigating slick city streets or stuff into a pack while hiking a trail is a wardrobe must. Likewise, a warmer layer for cold weather is invaluable and can take the shape of a puffy jacket or a sleek wool peacoat.

Depending on the sports or physical training you participate in, your clothing needs will differ, but basic layers with technically advanced properties are always appropriate.

Green Guide: This category is probably one of the greenest. Activewear retailers and brands are leading the charge in textile development and manufacturing. From Puma to Nike and Nau, nanotechnology and even 3-D printing are changing the way we dress and, in some cases, perform. Look for brands like Puma, who have factored their environmental costs into their overall profit-and-loss projections. They uphold a higher level of sustainability in their manufacturing. Recycled and upcycled material use is also a mainstay in this category, and everyone from Timberland to Patagonia (which has B-Corp status) is in on the action. Also, check out Nike's Better World range, and look for pieces that boast being "made in green" with recycled materials.

Another great way to go green is to shop secondhand. So many outdoors companies produce pieces that are made to withstand the elements and time. You can easily pick up an old pair of ski pants or a down vest that do their job without compromise—and save a bit of cash too.

WHO TO SHOP	INTEGRITY RATING	DIAMOND LEVEL	PRICE
Timberland	upcycled	eco-citizen	$$
Icebreaker	fair trade, transparent, natural fibers	eco-guru	$$
Patagonia	organic, recycled, transparent, fair trade, social	eco-guru	$$$
Engineered Garments	local	eco-citizen	$$$$
G-Star Raw	natural (and sustainable) fibers, fair trade, transparent	eco-guru	$$$

Reading through this chapter, you may have realized that there are gaps in your closet and pieces you'd like to add. Use the space below to make a list. By being clear about what you need (versus simply what you like) you'll be able to construct a more balanced and working wardrobe.

ITEM	POTENTIAL BRANDS	INTEGRITY RATING	DIAMOND LEVEL

Building a diverse wardrobe that supports your style and ethics is personally rewarding with effects that ripple outward. Just as you make educated choices with the food you eat, the energy you use, and transport you take, your wardrobe has a significant place in the lifestyle you create: a lifestyle that communicates who you are and what you support. With your integrity factors and Diamond Diagram in place, you'll confidently build that lifestyle. And, who knows, maybe even help to change the world with your wardrobe.

I hope you found this chapter useful and will check it as a resource to inspire your brand purchases when you add to your wardrobe. That concludes the clothing component for men. If you haven't picked up on it yet, this book is like a game of Chutes and Ladders. I now invite you, gentlemen, to skip ahead and slide into the last chapter (Chapter 10) for a crash course on nontoxic personal care products. Ladies, don't miss the next chapter—it is all about eco-fashion in action!

PART
3

CHAPTER 9

WOMEN'S SUSTAINABLE FASHION IN ACTION

"I wear my sort of clothes to save me the trouble of deciding what to wear."

—KATHARINE HEPBURN

Regardless of your soaring self-esteem or clear-cut style, everyone likes to be told what to wear now and again, especially when an invitation arrives and you're expected to dress accordingly. When you wear something that is absolute perfection for a specific occasion, your confidence and personal power cannot be contained, and that's hot! From black-tie weddings to backyard barbeques, this chapter will give you tried-and-true style tips for dressing the part.

Best of all, these occasions provide the perfect opportunity to spread the wear-no-evil philosophy by leading by example. When you receive a compliment on your outfit, you can tell the backstory of why you love what you are wearing too and perhaps inspire others to create the same confidence in what they wear and how it aligns with their ethics.

FASHION ME GREEN

When I first started FashionMeGreen.com, my vision was to build a visual platform to show women they didn't have to sacrifice style to be sustainable. I traveled the world and created editorial spreads like those of a major fashion magazine by organizing eco-fashion makeovers with leading style influencers. I worked with a PR director from Style.com, the fashion director from *Tank* magazine, and the enterprising founder of Independent Fashion Bloggers (just to name a few). For each city I visited I would contact these style influencers who were recognized for their impeccable style and taste, and I would ask them whether they were interested in being "fashioned green." They were always delighted by my invitation and excited to see how their personal style (based on what inspires them and the city they live in) would be represented with eco-alternatives.

Over the course of a week I would spend time chatting with them about their style and what influences their ensembles. After getting a good sense of their personal fashion taste I'd begin my hunt for eco-fashion designers and pieces based within their city to fulfill their sartorial requirements. By visiting designer showrooms and studios, I'd learn the backstories to their lines and pull pieces for the upcoming shoot. At the end of the week, with the help of a talented crew of professionals, we'd shoot the five-outfit spread with our style influencer as the model. Time after time the style influencer would squeal with joy and enthusiasm, moving from look to look and learning about the eco-initiatives behind the fabulous pieces they were modeling. By the end of the shoot they each had a few favorites that I am certain became beloved items in their own working wardrobes.

With these eco-fashion makeovers I always knew that my job was done when I heard the line, "Wow! There are so many pieces that I would gladly incorporate into my wardrobe, and I love that they are also eco!" Mission accomplished. Each shoot brought awareness to how easy it is to bridge the gap between style and sustainability without sacrifice. You know what they say: a picture is worth a thousand words. And these eco-fashion editorials became my case in point!

So now it is your turn to be fashioned green. The following eco-outfits are stylish looks that are perfectly suited for their corresponding occasion. With both style advice listed and an eco-option for how to get the look (including the integrity rating and diamond level), you can use them as a guide and resource. Then make them your own by adjusting them to the season, your surrounding environment, and signature style. And, as a special bonus, I've asked some of my favorite real-life style influencers to weigh in with their personal advice on what to wear where.

WEAR NO EVIL IN ACTION

Cocktail Party

Cocktail parties can range from wine tasting get-togethers at a friend's house to corporate-sponsored events linked to the launch of a new product or even the company holiday party. Ideally, what you wear to the office can easily be transformed into a cocktail outfit with a change of shoes, bag, and a swipe of lipstick. This is where the LBD comes into play and never lets you down. The cocktail party outfit is a balance of being sexy yet sophisticated. You don't have to be overly conservative in your attire, but keep things in check (no plunging necklines or cheek skimming minis). Depending on the occasion—is it corporate or casual?—you should keep your hair down to soften the look. Otherwise, a classic chignon bun is always elegant. The cocktail ring didn't get its name for nothing! Don't be afraid to don some statement jewelry.

Eco-Outfit: Go for a sequin top with a cropped black cigarette pant and heels. Add a blazer, statement earrings, and a clutch, and you are good to go!

ITEM	WHO TO SHOP	INTEGRITY RATING	DIAMOND LEVEL	PRICE
sequin top	What Goes Around Comes Around (vintage store)	secondhand	eco-citizen	$$
black slim pant	Theory	local	eco-citizen	$$$
blazer	Ekyog	organic, ethically made	eco-warrior	$$$
classic pump	Olsenhaus	vegan, fair trade	eco-warrior	$$$
earrings	Kevia	sustainable materials, social	eco-warrior	$$
clutch	Pele Che Coco	upcycled	eco-citizen	$$

Or Try . . .

A body-con dress (with a modest chest and a skirt length that hits between midthigh and your knee) with a cropped leather jacket, platform pumps (without an ankle strap—keep that leg looking long!), and an oversized clutch.

Or a puffy-skirt party dress. This may be better suited to a festive cocktail party and looks great with black tights and pumps, but you can also go for a bare leg and metallic heels (depending on the weather). Finishing touches include sparkly stud earrings, a small shoulder-strap bag, and a cropped tweed cardigan jacket with a Chanel-like feel.

Travel

Traveling is a tricky style situation. You want to look both put together (you never know who you might sit next to!) and simultaneously be comfortable for the many hours that go with the territory. The key is to wear layers made from comfortable and forgiving fabrics and to top things off with a touch of fashion flair with your accessories (like a great carryall tote and a flexible chic hat). Also, I have been lured by my inner fashion

diva to wear heels while traveling, justifying it by telling myself I won't have to walk that far and I will feel so much more chic—wrong! Some of these airports have you walk miles from your gate to ground transportation (London Heathrow, anyone?), and you will always be grateful for the added legroom you get from wearing a pair of flats. My advice is to always opt for a stylish pair of flats that you can slip on and off (pack a pair of socks in your handbag for the flight, and you will be stylish *and* smart).

Style Influencer: Caroline Issa, fashion director, *TANK* magazine and founder of BecauseLondon.com, London

Caroline is a Canadian transplanted firmly in London. She is a key supporter of young designers and consults for luxury fashion and retail brands. As a leading fashion influencer, Caroline travels the world on the fashion week circuit, continuously attending runway shows and presentations. As a woman who is always on the go and whose style is captured by the likes of *Vogue* and any number of fashion blogs, her style advice on what to wear while traveling is invaluable.

Style Advice

"Given I travel so much around the world for my job, comfort on a plane is key. I tend to invest in cashmere for travel and make sure I layer, as plane temperatures vary so much. I'll wear a comfortable, airy pair of cords along with a thin long-sleeve T-shirt and a cashmere sweater. And as much as I love heels, flats are the way to go when lugging around your bags!"

Wear-No-Evil Focus

"I am very interested in and inspired by labels who focus on sustainable processes in manufacturing. I am currently obsessing over the labels Maiyet and Study NY, both doing their bit to manufacture with local experts and change the way we think of fashion labels."

Eco-Outfit: Legging pants (they do exist, and they provide more shape in a thicker fabric), a longer V-neck tee topped with a fitted blazer and a scarf, finished off with a pair of ballet flats, sunglasses, and a large carryall handbag. Opt for dainty jewelry like a couple of layered necklaces to complete the look.

ITEM	WHO TO SHOP	INTEGRITY RATING	DIAMOND LEVEL	PRICE
T-shirt	Stateside	natural fiber, local	eco-warrior	$$
legging pant	Eileen Fisher	local	eco-citizen	$$
fitted blazer	Mango	made in green	eco-citizen	$$
scarf	Front Row Society	natural fiber	eco-citizen	$
ballet flats	Melissa Plastic Shoes	recycled plastic	eco-citizen	$$$
sunglasses	Waiting for the Sun	fair trade	eco-citizen	$$$

Or Try . . .

Ankle-skimming skinny jeans and a T-shirt, layered with a chambray shirt, fitted leather jacket, striped scarf, and a pair of slip-on sneakers.

A maxi dress with an open front, cozy-style cardigan, cinched in with a belt, and paired with flat T-bar sandals, a straw fedora, and a canvas tote. This is a great option for summertime travel or for when you are headed to warmer weather.

FIRST DATE

A first date can be that magical moment when it all began, and wearing the right outfit to help you show off your best self plays an important role. On a first date you'll want to look like you put some thought into your outfit, but also approached it from a relaxed and confident place. That translates to putting something together that you might wear to a job interview, and then taking it down a notch or making it more fun with accessories that are more casual. This is especially true for a daytime date, where a flat or wedge espadrille is better suited than a towering stiletto. Small cross-body bags are perfect for the first date, as they keep your hands free and leave you ready for wherever the date may take you.

Eco-Outfit: A soft and flirty dress that keeps you covered up on top while showing off a little leg (don't give it all away at once!), belted, with a pair of gladiator heels and a cropped blazer or bomber jacket. This is a great first-date outfit choice. It shows that you put thought into what you wanted to wear while kept things relaxed and approachable.

ITEM	WHO TO SHOP	INTEGRITY RATING	DIAMOND LEVEL	PRICE
dress	Dagg & Stacey	upcycled, local	eco-warrior	$$$
cropped blazer	H&M Conscious Collection	recycled polyester	eco-citizen	$$
heels	Coclico	veg dyes, fair trade, local, recycled	eco-guru	$$$$
purse	Matt & Nat	vegan	eco-citizen	$$
belt	Brave Leather	veg dyes	eco-citizen	$$

Or Try . . .

Colorful cropped jeans with an untucked voluminous blouse (think florals or embroidery), paired with wedges and a hobo bag. Layer a few necklaces for a finishing touch. Try this look for a daytime date.

A floral A-line dress with black opaque tights and black pumps, paired with a cropped blazer and stand-out earrings.

WEEKEND AND ERRANDS ATTIRE

The key to weekend dressing is to create a relaxed outfit without looking sloppy. In my opinion, beachside ladies do it best. The key is to have plenty of easy options (like tees and casual dresses) to pull a look together effortlessly. Flats are also appropriate here. On the weekend you'll likely be running errands or meeting up with friends to walk around a farmer's market or do some shopping, so a pair of flat sandals or sneakers is ideal. Make use of a shopper bag as your casual carryall, and create your own cool factor with a signature pair of sunglasses.

Style Influencer: Lina Hanson,
celebrity eco-makeup artist and author of *Eco-Beautiful*, Los Angeles

Lina is so sweet and humble, so I have to do the bragging for her here. She has a celebrity clientele of dedicated actresses such as Natalie Portman and Cameron Diaz, and she helps these starlets get ready for their various events while upholding her commitment to nontoxic beauty. Check out her book for all her beauty secrets! Her latest creation is her skincare brand, Lina Hanson. She sources natural ingredients from all around the world to create products that work for all skin types and ethnicities. Originally from Sweden, Lina has fully embraced the laid-back look of a California girl while also infusing a European-cool vibe. Her balance of casual and cool is perfect for meeting friends for brunch on Sunday or a day out shopping.

Style Advice
"Ever since I moved to Los Angeles I dress pretty casually. My style is somewhat eclectic. I like to mix some vintage pieces with newer stuff, and I also love accessories! A pair of jeans, vintage boots or TOMS, and an oversized top with my aviators is usually my go-to outfit for a day running errands."

Wear-No-Evil Focus
"I try to be conscious of recycling as much as possible. I keep my closet pretty simple. Every six months I go through my closet, and if I see something I haven't worn in a year, then I donate it. I also try to buy organic as much as possible, and whenever I travel I try to go to the local markets to find unique pieces like jewelry or handbags. I like this because it also helps to support the local artisans!"

Eco-Outfit: Skinny jeans paired with a striped tee, an anorak, scarf, and sunglasses. Ankle boots and an everyday tote round out the look.

ITEM	WHO TO SHOP	INTEGRITY RATING	DIAMOND LEVEL	PRICE
skinny jeans	Monkee Genes	organic, fair trade	eco-warrior	$$
tee	Stewart+Brown	organic, natural fibers, local	eco-guru	$$
jacket	White Tent	local, natural fibers	eco-warrior	$$$$
sunglasses	Gucci	sustainable materials	eco-citizen	$$$
tote	Fleabags	organic, natural fibers, vegetable tanned leather, local	eco-guru	$$$$
scarf	LemLem	social	eco-citizen	$$
boots	Timberland (Earthkeepers Collection)	upcycled	eco-citizen	$$

Or Try . . .

Oversized knit sweater with a jean miniskirt and slip-on sneakers. Add a canvas bag and sunglasses.

Maxi skirt with an easy tank tucked in. Layer on a cropped leather jacket, and add colorful flat sandals. Pair with a medium cross-body bag.

JOB INTERVIEW

Going in for an interview is both exciting and nerve wracking! Take the stress level down by securing a great look that oozes confidence while also hitting all the marks in accordance with the desired workplace environment. A foolproof way to dress for an interview and come off as professional (instead of looking like you're on your way to a cocktail party afterward) is to wear a looser-fitting dress that hits around your knees and then belt it. A fitted blazer and pair of closed-toed heels seal the deal. Also, don't forget to tend to your nails. Manicured nails polish off the look and can add a touch of color to an otherwise neutral outfit.

Eco-Outfit: Pair a colorful or printed top with a high-waisted skirt (which, lengthwise, hits below your midthigh), add a boyfriend-style blazer (roll the sleeves) and a belt, and finish off the look with a watch and some layered bracelets. Final touches include a pair of closed-toed pumps and a structured bag.

ITEM	WHO TO SHOP	INTEGRITY RATING	DIAMOND LEVEL	PRICE
top	Valentine Gauthier	natural (sustainable) fibers, fair trade, social	eco-guru	$$$
skirt	Amour Vert	natural fibers, local	eco-warrior	$$
blazer	Svilu	natural fibers, local	eco-warrior	$$$$
pumps	Cri de Coeur	vegan	eco-citizen	$$$
belt	Elvis & Kresse	upcycled, social	eco-warrior	$$
bag	Gunas	vegan, local	eco-warrior	$$$

Or Try . . .

High-waisted trousers, belted, with a silky tank underneath and topped with a cropped blazer. Stacked bracelets and a men's-style watch are perfect accessories. Add a structured tote and a pair of closed-toe platforms in an eye-catching color like blue or purple.

Slim-fitting black turtleneck sweater tucked into a knee-length black pencil skirt, belted with a wide statement belt. Semisheer hose and pointed-toe heels. Red lipstick and pearl earrings.

HOUSEWARMING OR DINNER PARTY

Parties hosted in someone's home are a special treat. They provide a more intimate setting and are usually more selective, creating a space for cultivating or nurturing friendships. For these intimate affairs you'll want to balance both dressing up (to show respect for your host) and down (to fit into the easy environment of a home versus a trendy restaurant). Dressing for a dinner party is akin to dressing for a first date; you'll want to dress up by wearing something that is fundamentally you and displays your stylish confidence while still being comfortable and a touch laid back.

Style Influencer: Tania Reinert Shchelkanovtseva, cofounder of ABoyNamedSue.co (online eco-boutique), Hong Kong

Tania is likely one of the best things to ever hit the eco-fashion industry! Her signature style and high taste level bring that certain je ne sais quoi to the fashion with substance scene. She has cocreated an online shopping site that rivals the fashion authority of Opening Ceremony. She buys and sells clothing for the kind of woman she is and is friends with—a fabulous group of independent and fiercely clad females who care as much about fashion as they do the planet. At her sky-rise apartment in Hong Kong Central, she often hosts get-togethers and dinner parties to bring her favorite people together and indulge in great food (her second passion, behind fashion). If anyone can pull off the dinner party–chic look, she can!

Style Advice

"I am a big fan of silk skorts and tops. They are both masculine and feminine, delicate and practical. Skorts are more forgiving and flattering as well, but make sure to pick a length that most compliments your figure. You can dress them up easily with a statement necklace and a pair of good heels. I would go for print in spring and autumn, dark jewel colors in winter, and ivory or cream in the summer.

"My go-to outfit is simple tanned or nude strap heels (subtle and leg elongating), silk shorts (or a skort), and a print top, paired with a pendant necklace. Finish off with a loose ponytail and a jacket draped over the shoulders for a colder evening."

Wear-No-Evil Focus

"I always check where the pieces are made. I then look at the materials with which the piece was made: organic cotton, silk, recycled plastic—for me it is about the innovation and effort made by the designer to seek the most sustainable or low-impact textiles they could find."

Eco-Outfit: A great pair of skinny jeans with a fitted sweater, heels, and some statement jewelry is relaxed yet appropriate. What you wear depends on the theme (if there is one or if there is someone you are celebrating) or the group of people (are they more laid back, or do they like to dress up too?).

ITEM	WHO TO SHOP	INTEGRITY RATING	DIAMOND LEVEL	PRICE
sweater	Elroy	organic, natural fibers, fair trade	eco-guru	$$
shorts or skort	Svilu	natural fibers, organic, local	eco-guru	$$$
heels	Stella McCartney	vegan	eco-citizen	$$$$
statement necklace	Dannijo	local, social	eco-warrior	$$$$
embroidered clutch	Cuyana	natural fibers, social	eco-warrior	$$$

Or Try . . .

A faux or upcycled leather skirt with a sweatshirt top—sleeves rolled and collar embellished with studs or beads—paired with loafers (for a miniskirt) or platform sandals (for a longer skirt) and a vibrantly colored lip.

Silky pants with an easy cotton tank, jean jacket, turquoise jewelry, and wedge espadrilles.

OPENINGS AND FORMAL EVENTS

The days of getting really dressed to the nines for an evening out are pretty much behind us (locked in a past when women wore coordinating hats with their outfits and ball gowns to soirées), but there are still a few occasions when one can indulge. The opera, a themed ball, a premiere, and even a benefit dinner or fundraiser are all par for the course. For these occasions don't worry about overdressing—this is your chance to indulge in elegant evening wear. Break out the red lipstick, bejeweled clutches, and extravagant hair accessories! If you don't have a dress that suits the occasion, consider renting one.

Eco-Outfit: Try a Grecian-style dress, peep-toe heels, and a cropped combed-silk jacket or faux-fur stole. Keep your look modern (and a touch Rachel Zoe) by adding a wide belt and some trendy earrings.

ITEM	WHO TO SHOP	INTEGRITY RATING	DIAMOND LEVEL	PRICE
dress	Isoude	natural fibers, local	eco-warrior	$$$$
shoe	Gwendolyn Carrie	upcycled	eco-citizen	$$$$
faux fur vest	Michael Michael Kors	vegan	eco-citizen	$$$
jewelry	Dirty Librarian Chains	upcycled, local	eco-warrior	$$
clutch	Kayu	upcycled, fair trade	eco-warrior	$$$

Or Try . . .

A full (floor-length) skirt with a crisp, white collared shirt and a wide belt (very Carolina Herrera). Add D'Orsay heels, pearls, and a sequin clutch for a more formal fundraising event.

Silk strapless jumpsuit, belted, with pointed-toe heels and a fitted tuxedo jacket. Red lipstick and diamonds are a given.

REUNION OR INDUSTRY EVENT

Whether you are headed to your high school reunion or an annual work conference, you'll want to look your best and most successful. The key is to create a classy look that is still in alignment with your personal sense of style and line of work. You want to come off as confident without trying too hard. Choose a dress from your closet that is a go-to piece for you, something you always feel great in. You can keep one part of your outfit flirty and fun (like a beaded jacket or a voluminous skirt) while balancing out the rest with a refined feel.

Style Influencer:
Christine Morris Bullock, buyer at Anthropologie, New Jersey

Spending her career as a buyer in the fashion industry—for many years at Barneys New York and most recently at Anthropologie—has allowed Christine to work with many talented designers and develop personal style that seamlessly oozes from her every outfit. She finds eco-friendly collections particularly exciting and loves being able to provide customers with stylish yet sustainable options.

Style Advice

"For a high-profile event I always like to incorporate one favorite new trend into my personal style. Start with something timeless rather than several trend pieces that can be distracting. I love dresses, so I would wear a fit-and-flare style in a neutral color palette. Add an of-the-moment handbag, high heels that are beautiful but wearable, several fine jewelry pieces, and one modern costume jewelry piece in line with the latest trends."

Wear-No-Evil Focus

"Fair trade is the most important aspect of sustainable fashion to me."

Eco-Outfit: A great fitted shift dress is the quintessential piece for imparting sexy confidence in all the right ways. Choose a dress that hits at the knee and hugs your body. Pair with classic pumps, a few stacked bangles, and a clutch.

ITEM	WHO TO SHOP	INTEGRITY RATING	DIAMOND LEVEL	PRICE
fitted dress	David Peck CROP	natural fibers, local, social	eco-guru	$$$$
classic pump	Lulu's (Vegan Shoes category)	vegan	eco-citizen	$
bangles	Mikuti	recycled, organic, social	eco-guru	$$
clutch	Calleen Cordero	natural materials, veg dyes, local	eco-guru	$$$$

Or Try . . .

A statement skirt with a tailored tank and cropped blazer (buttoned). Add classy heels and a small purse with a chain strap. A couple of cocktail rings finish the look.

A pant suit, tailored and in a quality fabric. Choose a feminine tank to layer underneath, pointed-toe stilettos, and an oversized clutch. Don't forget to wear a couple of key pieces of quality jewelry, like diamond earrings and a signature bracelet.

BARBEQUE OR PICNIC

These warm-weather outings take on a carefree feel and provide the perfect occasion to dress down in a cool and casual way. Think maxi dresses, cutoffs, and hippie vintage blouses. Also, because you know you will be at a park or traipsing around on someone's lawn, always wear either a flat or a wedge, which will give you more surface area with which to navigate uneven terrain. Sun hats and glasses are an excellent finishing touch.

Eco-Outfit: An oversized silk blouse tucked in at the front of a pair of cut-off jeans shorts and paired with flat sandals. Wayfarer-style sunglasses and a cross-body satchel bag complete the casual feel.

ITEM	WHO TO SHOP	INTEGRITY RATING	DIAMOND LEVEL	PRICE
silk blouse	Carrie Parry	natural fibers, local	eco-warrior	$$$
jean shorts	Levi's Water<Less	fair trade, reduced water footprint	eco-warrior	$$
sandals	Aspiga	natural fibers, social	eco-warrior	$$$
sunglasses	TOMS Eyewear	social	eco-citizen	$$
satchel bag	Erin Templeton	local, recycled	eco-warrior	$$$

Or Try . . .

A sundress with a fitted jean jacket, a canvas bag, and a pair of sandals.

A pair of army green cargo pants (cuffed) with a white tank and an embroidered cardigan. Add flip-flops and an easy leather tote.

WEDDING

Most weddings occur in the warmer months, giving greater options when choosing what to wear. However, never wear white—that is the bride's job. Check the invitation to discern the requested dress code, and if you have any questions, get in touch with the bride to clarify. A more formal (black tie) wedding calls for an evening gown. Garden party weddings are more relaxed, so long floral dresses in quality fabrics (like silk, chiffon, and lace) are picture perfect. If the invitation states that the dress code is smart casual or cocktail cool, you can wear a cocktail dress with fancy heels and a couple of key pieces of jewelry. A wrap and a clutch bring it all together.

Style Influencer: Jessica Quirk, fashion blogger and author of *What I Wore*

Jessica Quirk is a blogger and author with a mission to help women "Look Good, Feel Good." A former fashion designer, she began posting daily photos of her outfits online in 2007. Those posts became *What I Wore*, a personal style blog that now gets nearly 1 million views per month. In her blog and her book Jessica offers advice and inspiration for putting together outfits that help women feel confident, positive, and ready to take on the world.

Style Advice

"Summer weddings are one of my favorite occasions to dress up for. What you wear will depend on the setting and time of day of the wedding—afternoon weddings tend to be a little less formal than evening weddings. Avoid black, and go with a print or colorful cocktail or day dress. Remember, you can always dress up a simple frock with your hair, makeup, and jewelry and dress down a sophisticated dress with more relaxed styling.

"My go-to outfit is a printed dress, nude pumps, skinny belt, and a glam clutch or bag."

Wear-No-Evil Focus

"I'm most environmentally conscious when it comes to what I eat, and I buy as much of my food as possible from local farmers (plus it tastes better!). From a fashion perspective I like buying secondhand and vintage clothes because it's less wasteful, better quality, and unique."

Eco-Outfit: Try a long print day dress with strappy heels, and make it more casual with a belt, or keep it dressed up with statement jewelry and an easy clutch.

ITEM	WHO TO SHOP	INTEGRITY RATING	DIAMOND LEVEL	PRICE
dress	100% NY	local, fair trade, natural fibers, upcycled	eco-guru	$$$$
strappy heels	Stella McCartney	vegan	eco-citizen	$$$
box clutch	Suzanna Valerio	upcycled, local	eco-warrior	$$$
jewelry	Lizzie Fortunado	upcycled, local	eco-warrior	$$$

Or Try . . .

A classic cocktail dress with a modest bust. Coral or turquoise dangle earrings make the look more summery and casual. Pair with heeled sandals and a metallic clutch.

Pastel party dress with a voluminous skirt, lace or sequin bolero shrug, nude heels, and a contrasting color clutch.

As I mentioned, all of these outfit ideas are here to inspire you and help get your creative juices flowing when you are standing in front of your closet and can't decide what to wear. Make them your own, and if you are building your wardrobe, the Who to Shop column will definitely come in handy!

Don't let your fashion inspiration stop here, either. I constantly check out style blogs, look books, catalogues, and editorial spreads in my favorite magazines for updated ideas on what to wear. Creating personal style is a lifelong process, so keep it fun and keep exploring!

CHAPTER 10

BEAUTY BASICS

"For beautiful eyes, look for the good in others; for beautiful lips, speak only words of kindness; and for poise, walk with the knowledge that you are never alone."

—AUDREY HEPBURN

Bringing beauty into a wear-no-evil lifestyle is much more than just the icing on the cake; it is an essential part of completing a look and communicating your personal identity. Even the everyday products you use to cleanse, smooth, moisturize, and maintain your skin, hair, and nails have an important place in your routine. This chapter is all about extending the wear-no-evil mindset to your bathroom cabinet.

Whereas the Integrity Index and Diamond Diagram helped you identify and support the positive pieces and processes that make up a fashion item, discovering clean grooming products shifts the focus in the opposite direction. Now we are on the lookout for ingredients and methods (i.e., animal testing) that we *don't* want associated with our purchases and products.

According to the Environmental Working Group, in the United States the average woman uses twelve or more combined cosmetic and personal care products every day. The men's grooming product market is expected to grow to $6.1 billion in the United States by 2017. With wonderful scents, colors, and enhancing properties, it is easy to accept them at face value—as an integral and beneficial addition to your daily routine. Unfortunately, there is an ugly underbelly to the beauty industry, one that secretly houses and promotes toxic chemicals that have been shown to cause allergic reactions, skin and lung irritation, asthma, and cancer (to name just a few).

Being aware of what you put on your body is just as important as what you put in your body. As your body's largest organ, skin has a permeable membrane that allows it to absorb the products you place on it. In one way this is exactly what you want it to do, especially if your skin is thirsty for moisture! However, because the products are absorbed directly into the skin, they bypass the liver and other detoxifying organs and enzymes that normally help cleanse what is being circulated in your body. Instead, whatever you choose to put on your skin goes straight into your bloodstream and is pushed throughout your body without being filtered.

What's worse is that we have relied on the Food and Drug Administration (FDA) to monitor and control the ingredients and their amounts in the products we use, but they are not actually safeguarding us. They operate by laws and guidelines that are outdated and state that "trace" amounts of declared toxic ingredients are certified as "harmless." What they neglect to acknowledge is that these trace amounts build up, producing what is called body burden, in which synthetic chemicals that we absorb over time build up as we carry them in our bodies. Yuck.

Furthermore, the FDA is not required to safety test ingredients or impose labels identifying ingredients known to cause allergic reactions, toxic or hormonal imbalances, and cancer. Instead, regulation and labeling is a collaborative effort between the FDA and the major corporations who produce beauty products. The two work together to find a "win-win" situation that works for them and their profitability and not for us and our health. Faced with the FDA's unfortunate indifference, it is up to us, the consumer, to move the needle on what we voice as acceptable to purchase and put on—and into—our bodies.

The goal of this chapter is to provide you with a little necessary knowledge about what is going on in the beauty industry. Even though it is pretty scary, I'm not trying to scare you; instead, I want you to gain awareness of what to look out for (the most harmful ingredients) and develop a new method for selecting products that really do make you beautiful, both inside and out.

GOOD, BAD, AND UGLY

The old adage "ignorance is bliss" may hold true for some situations, but in the case of treating your body and planet well, "knowledge is power." Learning about different ingredients and rating systems need not be an overwhelming task either; in fact, when you narrow it down to the basics, identifying both ingredients and products that are pure, organic, and truly natural becomes a breeze. Let's begin by looking at some of the very best ingredients that are being used as natural enhancers, stabilizers, and emulsifiers in some of the leading eco-beauty products on the market.

Good

When purchasing products, a great rule of thumb is to buy the product with fewer ingredients. With less ingredients present, you are less likely to experience irritation and you decrease the possibility of ingredients interacting with each other in unforeseen and sometimes toxic ways. Another general rule to follow is to classify ingredients as either certified organic or green chemistry synthetics. Green chemistry is a new development in the beauty industry in which nontoxic ingredients and products are synthesized and designed to degrade into environmentally friendly waste at the end of their lifecycle.

A good example of green chemistry at work today is the concentrated extracts present in products, such as caffeine from green tea or carotenoids from tomatoes. These extracts are removed using a supercritical CO_2 as a solvent, which, true to green chemistry standards, takes into account the process, use phase, and discarding of the final product, all with sustainability at the forefront. Green chemistry is still evolving and is primarily based on finding and supplying alternatives to the toxic synthetics created in the past. One of the easiest ways to identify a product that is either using green chemistry or openly omitting toxic chemicals is to look for declarations right on the product. Look for the statements listed on the following page.

NONTOXIC SYNTHETIC LABELING

no petrochemicals	no sulfates	no parabens	no synthetic fragrance
no synthetic colors	no TEA	no DEA	no glycols
no silicones	no phthalates	no petrolatum	no PEGs

As this sector of the industry evolves, we may even see claims on products clearly stating that they were developed using green chemistry. Until then, stick to the list above to support green chemistry and avoid toxic synthetics.

If green chemistry sounds too sci-fi for you, look to naturally occurring, organic ingredients and products. The use of organics as a safe and price-competitive alternative from the food we eat to the personal care and cosmetic products we use is ever increasing. From Europe to the United States, Japan, India, and Brazil, organic ingredients are flooding the market, which is good news for the natural beauty industry. Leading a healthy and conscious lifestyle has increasingly become important to people all over the world, and manufacturers are responding by replacing active ingredients in their products with organic, naturally occurring ones. Listed below are some of the more prominent organic ingredients you'll find in your favorite natural products.

ORGANIC INGREDIENTS IN PERSONAL CARE AND BEAUTY PRODUCTS

argan oil	tangerine	papaya	Mediterranean oils
wine	soybeans	grape seeds	coconut oil
rice bran and rice	white and green tea	lavender	ylang-ylang
clove	vanilla	sake	botanical colors
vegetable dyes	seaweed	minerals	clay

ORGANIC PRESERVATIVES AND STABILIZERS

chitosan-Inula helenium	eucalyptus	salvia	lemongrass
lemon tree complexes	grain and grape alcohol	vinegar	salt
allatoin	aloe vera	comfrey	horse chestnut
curcumin	date	grapeseed oil	chamomile
pomegranate	soya	black, green, red, and white tea	chocolate

Products that are listed as certified organic undergo third-party certification from any number of organizations. When a product is declared "organic," it must contain at least 70 percent certified organic ingredients. In the United States we look for the USDA organic certification. You may also see certification from the Soil Association, ECO-CERT, or the Organic Consumers Association, just to name a few. For a complete listing of organic products and their rating, visit www.organicconsumers.org/bodycare. With just a little knowledge you can confidently purchase products that adhere to your personal standards for living an eco-conscious and sustainable life.

Bad

Focusing on the positive and good ingredients is certainly my preference, but we must also touch on the bad ingredients so that we know what they are and how to avoid them. Dr. Samuel Epstein wrote a timely book in 2009, *Toxic Beauty*, in which he dives into great detail about the toxic ingredients lurking in our everyday products that are causing allergies, asthma, cancer, and other unnecessary side effects. I fully recommend his book to give yourself a broader and stronger understanding of the realities surrounding the mainstream beauty industry and its products that are endangering your health.

Instead of going into great detail, which Dr. Epstein does in his book, I'll simply use the table on the following page to outline some of the ingredients most commonly found in beauty and personal care products that you should avoid. When you familiarize yourself with these ingredients, you can begin to keep your eye out for them and make sure that the products you purchase are void of their presence.

TOP TEN TOXIC INGREDIENTS TO AVOID

INGREDIENT	USED IN	NEGATIVE EFFECT
Aluminum	antiperspirant	neurotoxin linked to breast cancer and other damaging health effects
"Ethanolamines": DEA (Diethanolamine), MEA (Monoethanolamine), TEA (Triethanolamine), ETA (Ethanonlamine)	emulsifiers and foaming agents; used in shampoos, cleansers, body wash, hair dye, etc.	hormone disrupters linked to forming nitrates and nitrosamines with carcinogenic properties, banned in Europe
Formaldehyde and Toluene	nail polish, antiperspirant, makeup, hair dye, eyelash glue	frank carcinogenic (declared by the International Agency for Research of Cancer), causes immunological toxicity, banned in Sweden and Japan
Parabens	preservatives; used in most personal care products	mimics the hormone estrogen, disrupts hormones and normal hormone processes, may be linked to breast cancer and DNA damage
Phenoxyethanol	organic chemical compound preservative; used in more personal care products	touted as the "natural" preservative, but produces notable developmental and reproductive toxicity
Polyethylene Glycol (PEGs), Propylene Glycol (PG), Butylene Glycol	makeup, lotions, soaps, shampoo, etc.	hidden carcinogenic, declared highly toxic by the EPA, PEG linked to 1,4-dioxane, a known carcinogenic
Sodium Laureth Sulfate, Sodium Lauryl Sulfate	foaming and cleaning agents; used in soap, shampoo, toothpaste, mascara, bubble bath	hidden carcinogenic, linked to severe skin irritation, eye damage (formation of cataracts), impairs proper hair growth
Talc	cosmetic powders, eye shadows, blushes, bronzers, baby powder, sunscreens	frank carcinogen, linked to ovarian cancer, respiratory toxin
Thimerosal, Merthiolate	mascara	toxic metals; lead and mercury
Triclosan	antibacterial ingredient; used in soaps, acne treatments, antiperspirants, lipstick	registered as a pesticide by the EPA, may disrupt thyroid hormones, concern over use and the formation of resistant bacteria (super-bacterias)

The top-ten list highlights those that are most common and, therefore, also most commonly avoidable to the trained eye. Like anything else, the more accustomed you become with them, the easier they will be to spot. I recommend you take a snap shot of the previous table on your smart phone so that you can carry it with you and have it ready for review when you need it.

Ugly

If the table from the "Bad" section is overwhelming to you, focus on just these four toxic ingredients as ones to avoid at all costs.

STEER CLEAR LIST

INGREDIENT	USED IN	NEGATIVE EFFECT	ALTERNATIVE
Talc	baby powder and personal feminine hygiene products (tampons, pads, diaphragms) and powder	linked to ovarian cancer	Burt's Bees Baby Bee Dusting Powder, $6
Powdered titanium dioxide	loose powder makeup as a whitening agent	respiratory tract cancer	Bare Minerals Mineral Veil Finishing Powder, $20
Oxybenzone, Octinoxate, PABA	toxic sunscreens	hormone disruptor, similar to estrogen, shown to be a feminizing agent in both males and females	The Honest Company Sunscreen SPF 30, $13.95
Paraphenylene diamin (PPD)	brown and black hair dyes	frank carcinogenic, specifically causes non-Hodgkin's lymphoma, bladder and breast cancers	Logona Hair Color, $13

With their significant side effects, steering clear of these known carcinogens could be the best thing you ever do. Luckily, it is becoming easier to replace the products normally containing these toxins with ones that do not and still enjoy their intended benefits.

BUILD A BASE

Because my Auntie Holly ran a beauty boutique in the Bay Area in California, I was the grateful recipient of many beauty products and samples. I started using an eye cream when I was fourteen! I honestly can attribute my youthful face not only to my parents and their awesome genes (thanks, Mom and Dad!), but also to the care I put into building a base for my skincare routine. Just like anything else, a proactive and preventative approach pays dividends later in life. By finding the right cleansers, exfoliants, and moisturizers and keeping up their consistent usage, you are investing in your skin and yourself. Not only are eco-friendly beauty products more pure and free of toxic synthetic chemicals, they are full of vitamins and powerful antioxidants that actually improve the condition of your skin.

To dive deeper into nontoxic beauty, I recommend you pick up a copy of *No More Dirty Looks* by Siobhan O'Connor and Alexandra Spunt for the dirt on what's really in our beauty products as well as recommended clean alternatives. Also, *Eco-Beautiful* by celebrity makeup artist Lina Hanson is a fabulous resource on proper skincare and makeup application, with loads of eco-friendly product suggestions that she uses regularly on A-list stars.

As you can see, natural beauty is a big topic that I will only touch upon briefly in this final chapter. Of course, I am happy to weigh in with my favorites, which span nontoxic potions, cruelty-free lotions, and certified organic formulas. You can find them in the following Clean and Simple Product Guides. Just as you've learned to choose your clothing based on the standards you uphold as most important, you'll want to exercise that same logic here. If you are vegan, products that adamantly forego animal testing and are 100 percent vegan will be a top priority. Others may focus on organic ingredients. Whatever your preference, I am happy to say that today you can find it. Remember to use the Skin Deep Cosmetics Database website (ewg.org/skindeep) to vet your selections with their researched toxicity rating system. It is an easy-to-use resource that will keep your conscience and body clear.

PRICE CHECK

For each of the Clean and Simple Product Guides, you'll find my favorite products listed along with their benefits and general prices. Use this key to better gauge these beauty enhancers' pricing.

$ - - - - - - - - - $0–$30

$$ - - - - - - - - $30–$75

$$$ - - - - - - - $75–$150

$$$$ - - - - - - $150+

CLEAN AND SIMPLE SKINCARE PRODUCT GUIDE

Cleanse

Clearing away the dirt and other environmental pollutants, such as air pollution, car fumes, and cigarette smoke, that can clog our pores and create an undesirable layer that sits on the skin is essential in this day and age. Some estheticians swear by cleansing the skin twice a day, once in the morning and once at the end of the day. I've found that rinsing my face with lukewarm to cool water in the morning and saving the cleansing for night, after a full day of being out in the elements, works best for me.

PRODUCT	SKIN TYPE	BENEFITS	PRICE
Marie Veronique Organics Exfoliating Cleanser	oily, blemish-prone, sun damaged	a gentle exfoliating cleanser to keep pores clear and break away dead skin cells	$$
Juice Beauty Green Apple Cleansing Gel	normal, aging, sun damaged	lightening, brightening, and tightening	$
Green People Gentle Cleanse and Makeup Remover	sensitive, dry, aging	luxurious cream enhances skin's softness and moisture while removing impurities	$$

Hydrate

Restoring hydration and balance to your skin after cleansing is important. Not only does locking in moisture help you fight off dull-looking skin, but most products also now contain ingredients to help you fight free radicals and create layers to seal your skin for added protection.

PRODUCT	SKIN TYPE	BENEFITS	PRICE
Derma-E Hydrating Night Creme with Hyaluronic Acid	normal, dry, aging	complete hydration, reduction of fine lines and wrinkles, plumps skin for younger appearance	$
Melvita Perfecting Cream	oily, combination	natural alpha hydroxy acids help keep skin clear, light moisture	$$
Nvey Eco Delicate Hydra Calming Moisturizer	combination, normal, dry, sensitive	helps reduce redness and even skin tone, maintains skin's natural balance of hydration	$$

Extra Hydration Plus Anti-Aging Face Oils and Serums

Oils have long gotten a bad reputation as a cause of clogged pores and problem skin, but evidence is showing that the exact opposite is true. Applying oils gives your skin the essential fatty acids it needs to provide an environmental layer to protect the skin. Research now shows that a compromised skin barrier (which pure face oils help heal) is a root cause of eczema, acne, and wrinkles. Concentrated serums also become key players when seeking to optimize skin health. Natural combinations with potent ingredients pave the way for smoother, younger-looking skin.

PRODUCT	SKIN TYPE	BENEFITS	PRICE
La Bella Figura Daily Elements Defense Face Oil	normal, dry, aging	cell nutritive, fights environmental damage, softens skin, promotes a healthy glowing complexion	$$$
Restorsea Renormalizing Serum with Vibransea Complex	combination, normal, dry, aging	lightens, brightens, improves skin tone and elasticity	$$$$
Pai Age Confidence Facial Oil	sensitive, normal, dry, aging	minimizes inflammation, optimizes hydration, packs in numerous vitamins and nutrients for restored skin health	$$$

Eye-Area Hydration

As previously mentioned, I was a big fan of eye cream from a young age. It is important not to overhydrate this area with normal moisturizers, as this can lead to heavy bags under the eyes, and to use a designated eye area cream. Incorporate the right product, designed for this delicate skin, once or twice a day, and use your ring finger to apply from the outer corner of your eye underneath to the inner corner (your ring finger is the weakest finger and ensures the gentlest application). Guys, eye creams are for you too (in twenty years you'll thank me)!

PRODUCT	SKIN TYPE	BENEFITS	PRICE
Earth Tu Face Anti-Aging + Restorative/Sea Buckhorn + Geranium Eye/Repair Serum	all	intense hydration, improves elasticity, combats aging with high concentration of antioxidants, promotes cell regeneration	$$
Tata Harper Restorative Eye Créme	all	protects delicate eye-area skin, firms, reduces wrinkles	$$$
Suki Eye Repair Balm	all	preventative product with long-lasting hydration	$$

Lip Hydration

If you are like me, you are addicted to lip balm. It may not be a certain brand or flavor, but the mere act of moistening your lips is a daily obsession. That's okay, because our lips need that extra moisture, especially before bed. Show your lips some love with these products.

PRODUCT	SKIN TYPE	BENEFITS	PRICE
S.W. Basics Lip Balm	all	fun flavors, smooth lips, hydration, natural ingredients, vegan	$
Intelligent Nutrients Certified Organic Lip Delivery Nutrition	all	packed with antioxidants, anti-aging, moisturizing, pure enough to eat	$
100 Percent Pure Organic Mint Lip Balm	all	deeply moisturizes and softens, 100 percent pure ingredients	$

Exfoliate

Exfoliating regularly is an essential piece for maintaining healthy and radiant skin. Our bodies are constantly turning over new cells and schluffing off the old ones. When you have a buildup of old skin cells, the skin can look dull and dead, and it may contribute to skin problems, such as acne. By using either a scrub, peel, mask, or all three, you effectively remove a layer of old skin and let new healthy skin put your best face forward.

Personally, I like to mix up the types of exfoliants I use. One week I may use a scrub, and later in the week I'll use a mask. You can play around and discover what works best for your skin. The important thing is to take Nike's advice and just do it so you can reap the benefits of a good skincare regimen.

PRODUCT	SKIN TYPE	BENEFITS	PRICE
Juice Beauty Green Apple Peel	oily, combination, normal, aging	"glycolic acid"-like results, cell turnover, healthy, even, brightened, and glowing skin, skin detox	$$
NUDE Skincare Miracle Mask	combination, normal, dry, aging	evens skin tone, refines pores	$$
One Love Organics Brand New Day Microderma Scrub and Masque	oily, combination, normal, aging	use one or two times weekly to deeply cleanse and purify skin	$$

Shave

Whether you are shaving daily or once a week, men and women alike are all after the closest shave. Shaving is one of the most important eco-exercises you can take on. When you shave, you essentially open the pores by cutting the hair follicle and allow for nasty chemicals to enter your bloodstream directly. Choose a clean and green formula to slather on, and it's smooth sailing.

PRODUCT	SKIN TYPE	BENEFITS	PRICE
REN Tamanu High Glide Shaving Oil	combination, normal, sensitive	nourishes skin, leaving it smooth and soft	$
Aubrey Organics Men's Stock City Rhythms Shave Cream	combination, normal, dry, aging	soothes and invigorates with pure ingredients	$
Weleda Shaving Cream	sensitive, normal, dry, aging	safest, sensitive formula, ultra nourishing	$

Protect

Although many of the products already mentioned have natural properties that help protect the skin, extended sun exposure calls for an extra layer of protection. Unprotected time spent in the sun may lead to premature wrinkles, discoloration, dark spots, and even melanoma. Luckily, there are many eco-friendly and nontoxic options to help protect your skin from harmful UV rays. Remember, when looking for a natural sunscreen, avoid these toxic ingredients: PABA, benzophenone, oxybenzone, and octinoxate.

PRODUCT	SKIN TYPE	BENEFITS	PRICE
MyChelle Dermaceuticals Sun Shield SPF 28	oily, combination, normal, sensitive	chemical-free protection in a lightweight formula that won't clog pores	$
The Honest Company Sunscreen SPF 30	sensitive, normal, dry, aging	one of the purest sunscreens, no nanoparticles, no chemicals, uses zinc oxide to offer broad spectrum protection	$
True Natural Broad Spectrum SPF 30 Baby & Family Water Resistant Sunscreen	sensitive, normal, dry, aging	safest, sensitive formula, gluten-free, nanoparticle-free, uses zinc oxide and titanium dioxide to protect	$

CLEAN AND SIMPLE
BODY CARE PRODUCT GUIDE

Cleanse

Joshua Onysko, founder of Pangea Organics, once told me that you don't need soap to get clean—just enough water to wash things away. I actually know many men who adopt this strategy and never use soap when they shower. Yet a nice-smelling, purifying, and sometimes moisturizing body wash does make the bathing process better.

PRODUCT	SKIN TYPE	BENEFITS	PRICE
Nubian Heritage African Black Soap Body Wash	all (specifically problem or combination skin)	gently purifying and exfoliating, balancing, moisturizing, subtle scent	$
Intelligent Nutrients Total Body Cleanser	all	invigorating mint scent, nutrient rich, moisturizing, use for both body and hair	$
Pangea Organics Italian White Sage with Geranium & Yarrow Shower Gel	combination, normal	invigorates, tones, uplifts, soothes, moisturizes	$

Hydrate

In a magazine article I read as a teen, a celebrity (now I can't remember who!) tastefully posed nude and shared her secret to looking so good: applying lotion to her entire body every day. And she didn't boast about using some rare lotion that one would need to remortgage the house in order to afford. Pure and simple, she just said that all you need to do is get your daily dose of moisture. To gracefully age as she did, I am prepared to follow in her moisturizer-loving footsteps.

PRODUCT	SKIN TYPE	BENEFITS	PRICE
Acure Organics Lemongrass + Moroccan Argan Oil Firming Body Lotion	all	restores skin's buoyancy, stimulates collagen production, moisturizes	$
Elemental Herbology Watermelon and Cucumber Body Moisturizer	all	lightweight, cooling (great for summer months), non-greasy, nourishing	$$
Elique Organics Whipped Cream	normal, dry, very dry	rich and moisturizing, enriches epidermis, softens skin, use on face, body, and hair	$$

Body Oils

Some people swear by body oils as the best form of moisture. Contrary to common sense, they can impart just the right amount of moisture and absorb directly into skin, leaving you hydrated to perfection without a greasy residue.

PRODUCT	SKIN TYPE	BENEFITS	PRICE
Bamford Rosemary Organic Body Oil	sensitive, normal, dry, very dry	invigorating and nourishing, made from 100 percent organic ingredients	$$
Evan Healy Sweet Blossom Hydrating Body Oil	all	calms inflammation, deeply moisturizes	$
Lina Hanson Global Body Serum	sensitive, normal, dry, very dry	nongreasy, rejuvenates skin, relieves dryness, improves elasticity	$$$

Exfoliate

Just as your face needs a purifying pumice regularly, so does your body, especially during winter months, when skin is flaky and regenerating. Using an at-home exfoliator makes me feel like I've created my own minispa. It is a wonderful way to indulge and take care of your body.

PRODUCT	SKIN TYPE	BENEFITS	PRICE
Aromatherapy Associates Enrich Body Scrub	normal, dry, very dry	encourages circulation, enlivens skin, smoothes, moisturizes	$$
REN Guernade Salt Exfoliating Body Balm	all	gently exfoliates, moisturizes, leaves skin glowing	$$
SkinnySkinny Organic Black Coffee Body Scrub	all	detoxifies and hydrates, stimulates circulation in the lymphatic system, sugar based	$

Treat

A change in environment, recovery from an accident (or even stretch marks), or perhaps the desire to create a certain look all warrant a little extra TLC in the form of a treatment product. The key is to apply them regularly as directed for a sustained period of time. More often than not, this dedicated practice will improve your skin's condition and create your preferred effect.

PRODUCT	SKIN TYPE	BENEFITS	PRICE
Josie Maran Argan Self-Tanning Cream	all	creates a healthy glow, sunless tanner, lightweight, no mess formula, hydrating	$$
Derma-E Scar Gel	scars, severely sun damaged	softens, smoothes, and diminishes scars and stretch marks, reduces discoloration from cuts and burns	$
Erbraviva Stretch Mark Cream	stretch marks	shea butter and sea buckhorn oil combat stretch marks, hydrates	$

Deodorant

The quest for an all-natural and still effective deodorant has been a long one. My feeling is that there are some formulas out there that work better on certain people than do others and vice versa. Don't be afraid to keep trying them until you find one that works. To help narrow your search, I recommend starting with the ones listed on the following page.

PRODUCT	SKIN TYPE	BENEFITS	PRICE
Herbal Magic Deodorant	all	controls body odor, helps with underarm wetness, great for sensitive skin	$
Dr. Hauschka Deodorant	all	hazel and sage absorb odor, won't clog pores, soothing	$
Soapwalla Deodorant Cream	all	highly effective, clay powders and essential oils help absorb odor, moisture and inhibit bacteria	$

CLEAN AND SIMPLE
HAIR CARE PRODUCT GUIDE

Cleanse

One of the best hair care secrets is to train your hair to not need a washing for two or three (four, if you can manage it!) days. When you get on that schedule your scalp has time to regulate the oils it produces, improving the overall health of your hair and scalp. For the days you do wash your hair, these are some of the best products out there.

PRODUCT	SKIN TYPE	BENEFITS	PRICE
Intelligent Nutrients Harmonic Shampoo	normal, dry, frizzy	harmonizing, nurturing, antioxidant rich, antiaging, smoothing	$
Acure Pure Mint + Echinacea Stem Cell Shampoo Volumizing	fine, thin, normal	build volume without creating buildup, supports keratin, lightweight moisture	$
John Masters Zinc and Sage Shampoo with Conditioner	normal, dry, flaky	an all-in-one product (great for guys), fights dander, normalizing, balanced cleansing with hydration	$

Condition

Keep split ends at bay with the right conditioner, and add shine plus manageability.

PRODUCT	HAIR TYPE	BENEFITS	PRICE
Yarok Feed Your Volume Conditioner	fine, limp, normal	promotes moisture, volume, and manageability	$
Evolvh UltraShine Moisture Conditioner	fine, normal	optimal moisture with amino and fatty acids, balances pH, adds shine and bounce	$
Alterna Caviar Replenishing Moisture Conditioner	normal, dry, damaged, colored	intensive hydration, repair, added silkiness and strength	$$

Style

A little product can go a long way, both in terms of the amount you use as well as the various looks you can create. I find that even a little beach wave spray adds that sea-salt texture and transforms my otherwise lifeless locks.

PRODUCT	HAIR TYPE	BENEFITS	PRICE
Alterna Bamboo Volume Weightless Whipped Mousse	fine, limp, normal	feather-light mousse adds thickness and lift, leaves hair bouncy, touchable, and soft	$
Josie Maran Bohemian Waves Argan Hair Mist	fine, normal, curly, dry	soft, textured waves, adds natural volume and shine	$
Aveda Air Control Hair Spray	all	lightweight yet effective hold, fabulous scent	$

Treat

Environmental factors (sun, wind, pollutants) can take their toll on your hair, not to mention the damage we do with heat styling and hair color! Take the time to love your locks with any of these treatments, which I recommend using about once a week.

PRODUCT	HAIR TYPE	BENEFITS	PRICE
Jason's Thin to Thick Energizing Scalp Elixir	fine, damaged, normal	fortifies hair, nurtures the scalp, gives soft, voluminous hair	$
Shea Radiance Revitalizing Hair Oil	normal, frizzy, curly, dry	increases circulation, nourishes scalp and hair	$
Rahua Omega 9 Hair Mask, Gluten Free	normal, dry, damaged	revitalizing treatment, gives lustrous, healthy hair	$$

CLEAN AND SIMPLE
NAIL CARE PRODUCT GUIDE

Polish

I love women who view their fingernails as accessories, because they can be exactly that—a complement to your outfit or a standout pop of color when you need it. Steer clear of the shellacs, gels, and press-ons; they cause extreme damage to your nails (regardless of what your manicurist says), requiring weeks to heal. Instead, opt for a more natural polish that is free from formaldehyde, dibutyl phthalate (DBP), and toluene, plus formaldehyde resin and camphor (i.e., five free).

PRODUCT	BEST FOR	BENEFITS	PRICE
Jin Soon	vibrant hues and modern classics in a five-free formula	on trend colors in rich hues, even coverage	$
Priti NYC Priti Flowers Polish	non-toxic nail line, five free	great basic colors, wears well, minimal smell, easily removed	$
Scotch Naturals Watercolors	nontoxic, made with water base, five free	diverse offering of rich colors, applies evenly	$

Remove

PRODUCT	BEST FOR	BENEFITS	PRICE
Scotch Soy Polish Remover	water-based polishes, nontoxic	extremely gentle, low to little smell	$
Piggy Paint Nail Polish Remover	water-based polishes, nontoxic	low odor, hypoallergenic, works on all polishes	$
Priti NYC Soy Polish Remover Wipes	travel, all nail polishes	great travel, nontoxic, biodegradable	$

CLEAN AND SIMPLE

ORAL CARE PRODUCT GUIDE

Never underestimate the power of a beautiful smile. To keep your pearly whites looking their best, choose an effective and safe toothpaste, add a rinse, and always floss.

Toothpaste

PRODUCT	BEST FOR	BENEFITS	PRICE
Green People Fennel Toothpaste	sensitive gums and teeth	fluoride-free, certified organic, antibacterial	$
Nature's Gate Creme de Mint	teeth cleaning, brightening	reduces dental plaque, brightens teeth, clean, fresh feeling that lasts	$
Lush Sparkle Toothy Tabs	travel	antibacterial, palette cleansing, perfect for travel	$

Rinse

PRODUCT	BEST FOR	BENEFITS	PRICE
Essential Oxygen Organic Brushing Rinse	aids oral issues, including whitening, pockets, receding gums,	animals, USDA organic, aids immune system, staves off bad breath	$

CLEAN AND SIMPLE
COSMETICS PRODUCT GUIDE

Gents, your final jump is ahead to the last section: Help Me Help You Wear No Evil. Ladies, virtually every product you use now that is not nontoxic has a parallel natural alternative that not only provides the same effective coverage, colors, and wear but also has added vitamins and pure plant ingredients. How's that for an added eco-bonus!

I like to think of cosmetics as beauty enhancers, and eco-beauty cosmetics really are just that. Various hues, application techniques, and ingredients help to highlight your natural beauty. Incorporating makeup and beauty trends into your style speaks volumes. By identifying both classic colors and techniques that work for your skin coloring and personal style while also experimenting with seasonal beauty trends, you quite literally put your best face forward.

As we all know, fashion is cyclical and always changing. Beauty clips along with seasonal trends at the same pace. Fortunately, beauty has a much more narrow range in which trends, application techniques, and colors actually change. Thus, just as you've built your wear-no-evil wardrobe foundation with quality pieces that work for you season after season, you can build a cosmetics foundation perfect for your everyday style and then add in some specialized products for a night out or specific occasion.

All too often women become frustrated with their same old look and wind up making a drastic change that doesn't quite work. I have definitely been there! What we don't realize is that just filling in our eyebrows with a pencil, using a bright lip color when we feel tired, or adding a touch of blush to our cheeks transforms our whole look. That is the beauty of beauty. Although I won't go into specific application techniques here (check out MichellePhan.com or KeikoLynn.com for fantastic makeup tutorials), I want to touch on all the products you may want to bring into your beauty routine for a natural or dressed up look and give you some eco-options to choose from.

Base

Create a "clean" canvas by priming your skin, evening out skin tone, concealing any blemishes or dark spots, and then set with powder.

Prime

Primers are a set of new products that have become very popular. They smooth skin (filling in fine wrinkles) and help to provide longer, more even wear from your foundation or tinted moisturizer. If you have an event (or photo shoot!), they are an absolute must.

PRODUCT	BEST FOR	BENEFITS	PRICE
Devita Prime Corrective Light Refracting Primer and Corrector	minimizing imperfections, creating a smooth surface	light refracting, enhances luminosity, evens tone, decreases appearance of wrinkles and pores	$
Jane Iredale Smooth Affair Facial Primer and Brightener	antiaging proactive treatment, smoothing skin	evens skin tone, minimizes pores, creates luminosity, brightens skin	$$
Mineral Fusion Face Primer	creates a clear canvas for application, full coverage base layer, extended makeup wear	mattifies, diffuses fine lines and appearance of pores, restores skins moisture	$

Even

Even out your skin tone with a tinted moisturizer, or create a flawless complexion with foundation.

PRODUCT	BEST FOR	BENEFITS	PRICE
100 Percent Pure Fruit Pigmented Tinted Moisturizer	evening skin tone, adding moisture, supplying nutrients	100 percent natural and pure ingredients, vegan, gluten-free, seven shades available	$$
Nvey Eco Moisture Rich Fluid Foundation	full coverage	evens skin tone and create a flawless base, moisturizes and blends extremely well	$$
Josie Maran Argan Tinted Moisturizer	medium coverage, all-in-one product	moisture, foundation, SPF all in one, infused with argan oil to hydrate and nourish skin	$$

Conceal

Whether you have an unwelcome pimple or need to cover dark circles, the right concealer can transform your look and is often the key ingredient to a fresher, younger-looking face.

PRODUCT	BEST FOR	BENEFITS	PRICE
RMS Beauty "Un" Cover-Up Concealer	lightweight, flawless coverage	light, moisturizing, can be layered, heals skin	$$
Bare Escentuals Well-Rested Eye Brightener	creating a bright-eyed look, setting coverage of blemishes	buffs on to diminish dark circles, creates an even, bright-eye area, provides SPF 20 protection	$
Vapour Organic Beauty Illusionist Concealer	even application, won't clog pores, covers dark spots and imperfections	moisturizes, brightens, diminishes appearance of fine lines, enhances healthy glow	$

Set

Use a light dusting of powder (preferably with a big powder brush for even distribution) to set your makeup and eliminate shine.

PRODUCT	BEST FOR	BENEFITS	PRICE
Lavera Mattifying Mineral Finish (Loose) Powder	flawless finish, protection from environmental pollutants, great for sensitive skin	gives airbrushed look and feel, soothes skin, packed with antioxidant protection	$
W3ll People Realist Satin Mineral Setting Powder	creating soft focus look, setting foundation, extending wear	controls shine, minimizes pores, protects skin from free radicals, sets makeup	$
Youngblood Mineral Rice Setting Powder	fighting shine, nourishing skin	smooth, matte finish, create barrier to protect skin	$

Contour

With just a swipe of bronzer, a smidgen of highlighter, and a pop of color from a touch of blush, transform your features to bring out your bone structure.

PRODUCT	BEST FOR	BENEFITS	PRICE
Jane Iredale So-Bronze	adding a healthy glow	So-Bronze #3 suits all skin tones, adds a hint of shimmer	$$
Josie Maran Argan Illuminizer	adding radiance, highlighting brow and cheek bones	brightens and bronzes skin, conditions and restores skin, works on all skin types	$
Revolution Organics Freedom Glow Beauty Balm	imparting a fresh-faced look	gives a health glow, adds color, easy to apply, use on eyes and cheeks, cream base	$$

Eyes

Through numerous makeup tutorials, I've learned that when it comes to applying your eye makeup, the eyeliner comes first. That way you can blend it into your lashes and then shadow for a natural look. After you've finished with your shadows and mascara, go back in and define the eye with a final coat if you're after a more dramatic or precise look.

PRODUCT	BEST FOR	BENEFITS	PRICE
La Bella Donna Eye Pencil	creating smudged lines, natural look	offered in staple colors that complement all eye colors, delivers rich color with staying power	$
Alima Pure Luminous Shimmer Eyeliner	dramatic looks, adding shimmer, precision, and blending, apply with brush	enriched with minerals to create rich colors, great for shadowing or a touch of shimmer near lashes	$
Jane Iredale Liquid Eyeliner	precision, cat-eyed look	saturated color, staying power, easy to apply, nonirritating, available in multiple colors	$

Eye Shadow

Subtly enhance or draw dramatic attention to your eyes with the right eye shadows. As a general rule, it is best to have three shades that you can use for shading and highlighting: a light neutral color, a medium neutral, and a darker color (used to create definition at the outer corner and along the lash line).

PRODUCT	BEST FOR	BENEFITS	PRICE
Nvey Eco Eyeshadow in 162	highlighting brow bone and inner-corner of eye	talc-free, soothing, rich pigment, enriched with vitamins, great for sensitive skin	$
Youngblood Crushed Mineral Eyeshadow in Kasbah	overall lid color, medium neutral color	works on most skin tones, adds color to complement all eye colors, made from 100% pure minerals, bold and radiant	$
Lumiere Cosmetics Eye Pigments in Sublime	contouring color, rich and smoky hue for outer-corner shadowing	matte, adds dimension, perfect for creating a smoky eye	$

Mascara

If I were stuck on a desert island and limited to just a few beauty products, mascara would be at the top of the list (just after sunscreen). A light application gives a hint of color and defines your lashes, and a few more coats adds volume and an intentionally defined eye.

PRODUCT	BEST FOR	BENEFITS	PRICE
Dr. Hauschka Mascara	definition and length	strengthens lashes, moisturizing, gentle, nonirritating, washes off with water, comes in three colors	$
Josie Maran GOGO Instant Natural Volume Argan Mascara in Pitch Black	full lash look, volume and length	nonclumping, long wearing, water resistant, builds thickness of lashes, moisturizing, supports hair growth	$
Kjaer Weis Organic Mascara	lengthening, long lasting	nourishing, ingredients sourced from organic farms, delivers definition, adds layers to lashes, refillable tube	$$

Lips

Whether you opt for a natural-looking gloss or a bold statement lipstick, the right products can help you give good lip service. In a work setting I like to sport a matte lipstick that is rich with long-lasting color. On weekends a tinted lip balm or lip gloss does the trick. A small swipe of color can bring out your eyes and help highlight your skin tone.

PRODUCT	BEST FOR	BENEFITS	PRICE
La Bella Donna Mineral Light Lip Colour	long wear, more pigment, rich color	protects lips from UV rays, adds intense pigment, long lasting, moisturizing	$
RMS Beauty Lip Shines	medium- to light-color coverage, enhanced lip color	adds shine, slight pigment enhancement, antioxidant-rich oils protect delicate lip skin	$
bareFaced Mineral Cosmetics Natural Lipstick	medium- to full-color coverage, noticeable pigment enhancement	buttery and moisturizing, variety of shades, no artificial colors, long lasting	$

Even though this chapter gives a simplified introduction to eco-grooming and beauty, I know it can be a lot to take in. Don't feel you need to replace all of your less-than-pure products all at once. Just be conscious about the new ones you bring into your home, and start to make the switch gradually. Your personal-care purchases will help you put your best self forward while protecting the beauty of our planet.

FROM NOW ON, WEAR NO EVIL

Congratulations! You did it. You made it through the *Wear No Evil* handbook (check out LiveNoEvil.com for updated content, inspiration, and resources). From identifying (through the Integrity Index) and choosing to positively support (with help from the Diamond Diagram) the issues that affect our wardrobes, environment, and the many people who produce the fashion we make our own, we become the new educated and influential ambassadors of style. Now it is up to you to take what you've learned and make it your own. That is the best part: each of us has our own style, image of ourselves, and encompassing lifestyle that we create. When you commit to wear no evil (across both fashion and beauty), you actively share your truer self with those around you. And when you make your preferences known by voting with the dollars you use to purchase products, brands listen and respond. Your commitment to buying organic and pesticide-free fabrics will play a role in decreasing the almost three million poisoning cases each year. Your stand to support fair trade and an ethical wage will make a difference in a community and the lives of those who, by being paid a little more for their work, will live a little better. Even the secondhand clothing you choose to incorporate into your closet or dispose of properly through textile recycling programs will play a part in reducing our overall CO_2 emissions. From this day forward remember: the small commitment you make on a personal level has a huge effect—an effect that ripples out, inspires others, communicates your standards, and shifts the world. So go ahead—change the world with your wardrobe, and wear no evil.

RESOURCE PAGES

HELP ME HELP YOU WEAR NO EVIL

Just in case you are thirsty for more or want to dive deeper into certain areas, here's a list of go-to resources that will help you on your journey to wearing no (okay, *less* might be a better word until the world becomes a perfect place) evil.

THIRD-PARTY CERTIFIERS

Environmental Working Group (ewg.org)

Skin Deep Cosmetics Database (ewg.org/skindeep)

Higg Index (apparelcoalition.org/higgindex)

Oeko-Tex Standard 100 (oeko-tex.com)

Global Organic Textile Standard (global-standard.org)

Bluesign Standard (bluesign.com)

Eco-Index (eco-index.org)

Nike's Material Choice and Impact site (nikeresponsibility.com/infographics/materials/index.html)

ECO-FASHION + NONTOXIC BEAUTY SITES AND RESOURCES

Live No Evil (livenoevil.com)

Sustainable Brands (sustainablebrands.com)

Ecouterre (ecouterre.com)

Fashion Me Green (fashionmegreen.com)

Ethical Fashion Forum (ethicalfashionforum.com)

Eco Salon (ecosalon.com)

The Guardian Environment Section (guardian.co.uk/environment)

Green Beauty Team (greenbeautyteam.com)

Organic Beauty Talk (organicbeautytalk.com)

No More Dirty Looks (nomoredirtylooks.com)

A Green Beauty (agreenbeauty.com)

Coco Eco Magazine (cocoecomag.com)

Sublime Magazine (sublimemagazine.com)

Conscious Magazine (consciousmagazine.co)

ONLINE ECO-BOUTIQUES

Zady (zady.com)

A Boy Named Sue (aboynamedsue.co)

Modavanti (modavanti.com)

Reve En Vert (revenvert.com)

Yooxygen (yoox.com/project/yooxygen)

Juno and Jove (junoandjove.com)

Kaight NYC (kaightshop.com)

Fashion Conscience (fashion-conscience.com)

ASOS GreenRoom (asos.com/women-green-room)

Maiden Nation (maidennation.com)

Latitude Global Give section (shoplatitude.com)

Fashioning Change (fashioningchange.com)

Helpsy (helpsy.com)

Made Collection (madecollection.com)

TOMS Marketplace (toms.com/marketplace)

Joinery (joinerynyc.com)

ONLINE ECO-BEAUTY STORES

NuboNau (nubonau.com)

Spirit Beauty Lounge (spiritbeautylounge.com)

Hip Apotheca (hipapotheca.com)

Detox Market (thedetoxmarket.com)

Embody Beauty (embodybeauty.com)

STYLE + BEAUTY INSPIRATION SITES

Cupcakes and Cashmere (cupcakesandcashmere.com)

Who What Wear (whowhatwear.com)

GOOP (goop.com)

The Blonde Salad (theblondesalad.com)

The Glamourai (theglamourai.com)

The Zoe Report (thezoereport.com)

Net-a-Porter (net-a-porter.com)

The Chriselle Factor (thechrisellefactor.com)

Style Saint (stylesaint.com)

Refinery29 (refinery29.com)

Into The Gloss (intothegloss.com)

Michelle Phan (michellephan.com)

Ann Street Studio (annstreetstudio.com)

Violet Grey (violetgrey.com)

Fashion Gone Rogue (fashiongonerogue.com

Darling Magazine (darlingmagazine.org)

NOTES

Chapter 1

1. Nina Garcia, *The Little Black Book of Style* (New York: Harper Collins, 2007), 5.

2. Elizabeth L. Cline, *Overdressed: The Shockingly High Cost of Cheap Fashion* (New York: Penguin, 2012).

3. Dana Thomas, *Deluxe: How Luxury Lost Its Luster* (New York: Penguin, 2008).

4. Cline, *Overdressed.*

5. Ibid.

6. "Textiles," US Environmental Protection Agency, www.epa.gov/osw/conserve/materials/textiles.htm.

7. Joe Karp, "Municipal Governments Throughout California: Begin a Textile Waste Recycling Program" (petition), Change.org, www.change.org/petitions/municipal-governments-throughout-california-begin-a-textile-waste-recycling-program-2.

8. Jason W. Clay, *World Agriculture and the Environment* (Washington, DC: Island Press, 2004), 288.

9. "It Takes 1,800 Gallons of Water to Make One Pair of Jeans," Water Use It Wisely, http://wateruseitwisely.com/it-takes-1800-gallons-of-water-to-make-one-pair-of-jeans/.

10. Greenpeace.org, *Toxic Threads: The Big Fashion Stitch Up* (Amsterdam: GreenPeace International, 2012), 13.

11. Ibid., 3.

12. Kate Fletcher and Lynda Grose, *Fashion & Sustainability: Design for Change* (London: Laurence King Publishing, 2012), 23.

13. Ibid., 21.

14. World Economic Forum, "More with Less: Scaling Sustainable Consumption and Resource Efficiency," 2012, www.weforum.org/reports/more-less-scaling-sustainable-consumption-and-resource-efficiency.

15. "Animals Used for Clothing," PETA, www.peta.org/issues/Animals-Used-for-Clothing/default.aspx.

16. Food and Agriculture Organization of the United Nations, Slaughtered/Production Animals 2008, FAOSTAT Database, April 14, 2010.

17. Doris Schubert, "Assessment of the Environmental Release of Chemicals from the Leather Processing Industry," *IC-07 Leather Processing Industry,* July 28, 1998.

18. Richard E. Sclove, Madeleine L. Scammell, and Breena Holland, *Community-Based Research in the United States: An Introductory Reconnaissance, Including Twelve Organizational Case Studies and Comparison with the Dutch Science Shops and the Mainstream American Research System* (Amherst. MA: The Loka Institute, 1998) 52.

19. "Wool, Fur, and Leather: Hazardous to the Environment," PETA, www.peta.org/issues/Animals-Used-for-Clothing/wool-fur-and-leather-hazardous-to-the-environment.aspx.

20. Carbon Trust, "Clothing," www.carbontrust.com/media/38358/ctc793-international-carbon-flows-clothing.pdf.

21. Alexandra Harney, *The China Price: The True Cost of Chinese Competitive Advantage* (New York: Penguin Books, 2009), 28.

22. Ibid., 16.

23. Ibid., 57.

24. Thomas, *Deluxe,* 204.

25. Bonnie Kavoussi, "Average Cost of a Factory Worker in the U.S., China and Germany," *Huffington Post,* www.huffingtonpost.com/2012/03/08/average-cost-factory-worker_n_1327413.html.

26. *EcoTextile News,* "Pollution—Holistic Approach Needed," February/March 2013, 55.

27. Sandy Black, "Ethical Fashion and Eco Fashion," in *The Berg Companion to Fashion,* ed. Valerie Steele, 251–260 (Oxford: Berg, 2010).

28. "Secondhand Clothing," Berg Fashion Library, www.bergfashionlibrary.com/staticfiles/Encyclopedia/Secondhand-Clothing-Global-Fashion.pdf.

29. Oxfam, www.oxfam.org.uk.

30. Traidcraft, www.traidcraft.co.uk.

31. PETA, www.peta.org.

32. Katharine Hamnett, Slogan T-Shirts, www.katharinehamnett.com/Campaigns/Slogan-T-Shirts.

33. Loretta Keane and Cheri Fein, "Eco-Fashion: Going Green," The Museum at FIT 2010, http://www.fitnyc.edu/7885.asp.

34. "Eco Fashion," *Vogue,* www.vogue.com/voguepedia/Eco_Fashion.

35. Ibid.

36. Black, "Ethical Fashion and Eco Fashion."

37. "Eco Fashion," *Vogue,* www.vogue.com/voguepedia/Eco_Fashion.

38. Susanne LeBlanc, "Sustainable Fashion Design: Oxymoron No More?" BSR, October 2012, www.bsr.org/reports/BSR_Sustainable_Fashion_Design.pdf.

39. Black, "Ethical Fashion and Eco Fashion."

40. Ibid.

41. Stella McCartney, www.stellamccartney.com.

42. Trash Couture, www.trash-couture.com/about.htm.

43. Gucci America, "New Packaging Is 100% Better," Gucci, http://www.gucci.com/us/worldofgucci/articles/eco-friendly-packaging.

44. "Eco Fashion," *Vogue,* www.vogue.com/voguepedia/Eco_Fashion.

45. Cotton, Fair Trade, www.fairtrade.net/cotton.html.

46. "Bono's Fashion Moment," *Vogue,* March 15, 2005, www.vogue.co.uk/news/2005/03/15/bonos-fashion-moment.

47. Linda Loudermilk, www.lindaloudermilk.com.

48. "About Estethica," British Fashion Council, www.britishfashioncouncil.com/content/1146/Estethica.

49. "Eco Fashion," *Vogue,* www.vogue.com/voguepedia/Eco_Fashion.

50. Ibid.

51. Rogan NYC, www.rogannyc.com.

52. "Eco Fashion," *Vogue,* www.vogue.com/voguepedia/Eco_Fashion

53. Jennifer Farley and Colleen Hill, curators, "Eco-Fashion: Going Green," The Museum at FIT 2010, www3.fitnyc.edu/museum/eco_fashion_going_green/exhibition.html.

54. "Eco Fashion," *Vogue,* www.vogue.com/voguepedia/Eco_Fashion.

55. Ibid.

56. Ibid.

57. Ibid.

58. Copenhagen Fashion Summit, www.copenhagenfashionsummit.com.

59. Local Sourcing/City Source, Fashion Sourcing Network, www.fashionsourceny.com/local-sourcing/city-source.

60. Livia Firth, "It Can Only Be the Oscars!" *Vogue,* February 27, 2012, www.vogue.co.uk/blogs/livia-firth/2012/02/27/oscars-2012.

61. "Targets," Kering, www.kering.com/en/sustainability/targets.

62. "PETA Kicks Uniqlo's Butt Again Over Cruel Sheep Mulesing," PETA, http://blog.peta.org.uk/2012/06/peta-kicks-uniqlo%E2%80%99s-butt-again-over-cruel-sheep-mulesing/.

63. "The Higg Index," Sustainable Apparel Coalition, www.apparelcoalition.org/higgindex.

64. Olivia Bergin, "Gwyneth Paltrow Collaborates with Chinti and Parker, *Telegraph*, September 21, 2012, http://fashion.telegraph.co.uk/columns/olivia-bergin/TMG9557697/Gwyneth-Paltrow-collaborates-with-Chinti-and-Parker.html.

65. Waste<Less, Levi's, http://us.levi.com/shop/index.jsp?categoryId=19071316.

66. Have You Cottoned On Yet?, www.cottonedon.org.

67. Detox Timeline, Greenpeace, www.greenpeace.org/international/en/campaigns/toxics/water/detox/Detox-Timeline.

68. Don't Let Fashion Go to Waste, H&M, http://about.hm.com/AboutSection/en/About/Sustainability/Commitments/Reduce-Reuse-Recycle/Garment-Collecting.html.

Chapter 2

1. Atul Kumar, Pratibha Choudhary, and Poonam Verna, "A Comparative Study on the Treatment Methods of Textile Dye Effluents," *Global Journal of Environmental Research* 5, no. 1 (2011): 46–52.

2. Fred Guterl,,"It's Too Late to Stop Global Warming," *Newsweek*, August 31, 2009.

3. "Pesticides in Groundwater," USGS, ga.water.usgs.gov/edu/pesticidesgw.html, September 2012.

4. Sonali Bhawsar, "Toxic Fibers and Fabrics," BioTechArticles.com, 2011, http://m.biotecharticles.com/Toxicology-Article/Toxic-Fibers-and-Fabrics-699.html.

5. Josef G. Thundiyil, Judy Stober, Nida Besbelli, and Jenny Pronczuk, "Acute Pesticide Poisoning: A Proposed Classification Tool," World Health Organization, www.who.int/bulletin/volumes/86/3/07-041814/en/.

6. Textile Recycling Association, textile-recycling.org.

7. Claudio Luz, "Waste Couture: Environmental Impact of the Clothing Industry," *Environmental Health Perspectives* 115, no. 9 (September 2007): A449–A454.

8. Beatrice Machado Krueger, Jasibe Guzman Mena, and Ankita Srivastava, "The Textile Industry and Water Conservation," Center for Sustainable Enterprise, https://extranet.kenan-flagler.unc.edu/kicse/ORIG%20Shared%20Documents/The_Textile_Industry_and_Water_Conservation.pdf.

ACKNOWLEDGMENTS

To my guru, Paramahansa Yogananda, thank you for your guidance and blessings.

Thank you to my mama, Tricia, whose selfless love has always nurtured me and allowed me to pursue my various paths. Many thanks to Tricia and my stepfather, Allan, for encouraging my education in sustainability and fashion and for your support during my writing process. Thank you to my dad, Danny, for sharing such a wonderful view of how the world works and for always encouraging me to follow my dreams. To my sisters, Natalie (meow) and Carly, thank you for always believing in me!

Thank you Josh Spear for being the first person to suggest I start a blog if I wanted to write a book. Your support and suggestions made this book possible. Thank you for investing in my personal growth by challenging me and encouraging me. Thank you for all your love and for being my rock. To the Spear family, thank you for your steadfast support, open arms, and inspiring influence.

Many thanks to Meg Thompson, my agent, for being the best agent out there (it sounds cliché, but I really mean it)! Thank you for seeing the potential for this book and holding my first-time-author hand throughout the process. And thank you for lending your creative juices and coming up with our awesome title!

Thank you to Cindy De La Hoz, my editor. Thank you for seeing the vision behind this book and fighting for its place in the world. Thank you to Carolyn Sobczak, my production editor, Josephine Mariea, my copy editor, Josh McDonnell, my cover and layout designer, Peggy Garry, for your legal expertise, and the entire Running Press and Perseus Books Group family for your collaborative editing and expertise—you truly turned this book into its best version, and I could not have done it without you.

Natasha Landenberger, thank you for being the incredibly talented illustrator you are and for taking a chance on a new project to work with me and help bring this book visually to life!

To all the brands, designers, writers, and supporters of style with substance, thank you for your commitment to bringing awareness and change to the world of fashion and beauty.

Lastly, I'd like to thank you, dear reader, for your curiosity and motivation to take a stand for sustainability and the world we are leaving for generations to come. Thank you for incorporating eco-awareness into your daily stylish lives and continue to lead by wear-no-evil example.

Index

I

J